DECADES

Curved Air

in the 1970s

Laura Shenton

sonicbondpublishing.com

Sonicbond Publishing Limited
www.sonicbondpublishing.co.uk
Email: info@sonicbondpublishing.co.uk

First Published in the United Kingdom 2021
First Published in the United States 2021

British Library Cataloguing in Publication Data:
A Catalogue record for this book is available from the British Library

Copyright Laura Shenton 2021

ISBN 978-1-78952-069-9

Typeset in ITC Garamond & ITC Avant Garde
Printed and bound in England

Graphic design and typesetting: Full Moon Media

DECADES

Curved Air

in the 1970s

Laura Shenton

sonicbondpublishing.com

DECADES | Curved Air in the 1970s

Contents

Preface

The first time I heard a Curved Air song, it wasn't actually Curved Air that I was listening to. It was actually the version of 'Back Street Luv' that was played by session musicians on Volume 19 of the *Top Of The Pops* LP issued by Hallmark Records. Such was the success of Curved Air quite early on in their tenure that, unusually perhaps for a progressive rock band, they captured the imagination of pop fans with the August 1971 release of their single of 'Back Street Luv'. The song was on their appropriately-titled, *Second Album*. But even their first album – *Air Conditioning*, released in November 1970 – had already made waves, grabbing the record-buying public's attention with a picture disc. Musically though, there was certainly something good going on. So much so that not long after the band had formed, they were signed to the Warner Bros. record label, but only after a bidding war. Warner Bros wanted Curved Air, and very much so. They were an exciting and innovative band.

Curved Air were active ultimately between the years from 1970 until their break-up in 1976. They made a significant contribution to music via several albums, varying in style. The band saw many musicians come and go, but there was always so much talent in every single line-up. Some of their musicians were classically trained, some weren't, but essentially, the level of talent was unquestionable.

It fascinates me that nobody has yet written a book about Curved Air, and in particular, what they achieved during the 1970s. It is for that reason that I am doing it. Their story needs to be told because it is interesting and worthwhile. Of course, as the author of this book, I am very much a fan of the band, but within that remit, I promise to put something out there that is informative and objective. This book is about Curved Air in the 1970s, and ultimately, I wasn't there, man! I was born in 1988: quite a while after the decade referred to in this book, and thus, it's a culmination of extensive research that I intend to use objectively in order to offer a constructive narrative on what is ultimately a very worthwhile band.

In the interests of transparency and context, as author of this book, I have no affiliation with Curved Air or any of the band's associates. As a result, you're going to see a lot of quotes from vintage interviews in this book. I think that's important because there's probably going to come a time when stuff like that gets harder and harder to find. It needs to be collated because Curved Air's contribution to music is certainly worthy of such archiving and, indeed, discussion.

Introduction

Curved Air were one of the most accomplished bands to come out of
Britain during the explosion of progressive rock. Their success was
such that they toured with Black Sabbath, Deep Purple, Jethro Tull
and Emerson, Lake & Palmer. They also shared bills with The Doors,
Steppenwolf, B.B. King, Johnny Winter and Dr. John.

Curved Air originated, partially, from a band called Sisyphus. Violinist
Darryl Way – a graduate of the Royal College of Music – formed the group
in early 1970 with two former members of Sisyphus: keyboard player
Francis Monkman and drummer Florian Pilkington-Miksa. Bassist Robert
Martin then joined. Violinist-extraordinaire, Way met Monkman in the
late 1960s during a visit to a music store when he went in to purchase an
electric pick-up for his violin: quite the advanced piece of technology at the
time. Francis Monkman happened to be in the shop when he heard this
great big noise coming from a tiny violin. It impressed him tremendously.
Both Monkman and Way came from a classical training background but
were very much into the experimental rock music that was thriving during
the late 1960s. Darryl Way has since referred to Keith Emerson's The Nice,
and Robert Fripp's King Crimson, as being inspirational in putting the idea
across that within rock music, there was scope for classical influences to
be included and that this was very much a strong remit within Curved Air.
Also fans of American band Spirit, Darryl Way and Francis Monkman had
a keen interest in taking their respective electric instruments – violin and
keyboards – beyond a basic extent of amplification.

In 1969 – upon the request from Galt MacDermot (who wrote the music
for the musical *Hair*) – Sisyphus, as they were still known, were recruited
as the pit band for the resident play at the Mercury Theatre in Notting
Hill Gate: *Who The Murderer Was*. Impressed with their fusion of rock
sounds, whilst working as a photographer for one of the shows, Mark
Hanau offered up his management services; he was keen to take the band
further. Upon hearing Sonja Kristina – a member of the cast of *Hair* – at
the Shaftesbury Theatre, Hanau and the band asked her to join them.
McDermot recommended that Kristina would be excellent to work with,
after the run of *Hair* had finished, of course. Before securing her role in
Hair, Sonja Kristina used to sing in folk clubs across London. She had a
very hippie bohemian sort of charisma about her: a wild child who stayed
out all night partying and playing music. Sonja Kristina mused in *Disc* in
April 1972:

When I went into *Hair*, I identified with it all completely – it was my way of life. Then with Curved Air I was working to the same type of audiences. The sex thing did come into it – the basic sex signals you don't realise you're doing were there, that's all.

In an interview with *Prog* in February 2018, Sonja Kristina was asked if she felt intimidated by the classical training of the other band members. She replied graciously:

Not at all. The fact they were so well musically trained made no difference to me. I liked their songs, and also the fact they were keen for me to write lyrics to fit. I love working with words. In general, I am not easily intimidated or overawed by people or situations.

She considered in *The Arts Desk* in April 2014:

I'm not a musician in the same way Darryl Way and Francis Monkman are. I didn't go to music college and learn about time signatures. My way of approaching music is to let people play freely around my songs, which are influenced by whatever's around me at the time. I can't write Curved Air music – except for 'Melinda (More Or Less)' kind of things – but I did write the lyrics, except for Francis' 'Piece Of Mind' and 'Over And Above'.

Eventually, the group chose the name Curved Air. The name was taken from a modern classical composition called *A Rainbow In Curved Air* by minimalist composer, Terry Riley. Francis Monkman had participated in the London premiere of Riley's well-known composition, *In C. A Rainbow In Curved Air*, would inform much of the band's early work. Sonja Kristina recalled in *Record Collector* in April 2012:

Thanks to Roy (Guest), I joined Equity (the actors' union). He also told me about the auditions. We all knew we were in a really ground-breaking show – the first manifestation of *Hair* outside the States. Galt MacDermot, the composer, had written another musical, *Who The Murderer Was*, and the rest of what became Curved Air were the pit band. Roy told me they were looking for a singer, and I auditioned with 'Melinda (More Or Less)', which was to be on *Phantasmagoria*.

In *Hit Channel* in December 2018, Sonja Kristina recalled her experiences of being in *Hair*:

When I sang it originally, I was just nineteen and it was very nerve-racking, as I was the only person on stage, after there having been a lot of activity on the stage. It was very well-received. I had to sing it the way the American cast did. *Hair* was a wonderful experience. I had done some drama at school, we did a couple of Shakespeare plays and then I did a drama exam. Then, I went to a drama college just for a year. I was lucky enough to get into the cast of *Hair*. The whole thing was about more energy, about filling as much space as possible on the stage with your energy and interacting with the rest of the cast with trust. We had to do some exercises where you'd fall back on different people and you had to trust that they will catch you. We'd spent time sitting in front of each other, just staring at each other and touching each other's face. The whole thing was to make us very, very natural on stage. When we performed, we had to perform with maximum energy. Every time we were coming up to the opening time, the writers of the play would say, 'More energy! More energy!' – It was a three-hour show, we did eight shows a week. So, I think I grew with this because I learned to be completely free, to be able to move very freely on the stage and to perform with great energy, to feel very at home with being on the stage and also at home with the audience and to create where I am, other than doing something rehearsed. In that way, it all made sense. That was what I gained from being in *Hair*. It was a fantastic experience! Very good. The best training I have ever had.

Still, though, it seems that what was eventually to become Curved Air came along at the right time for her. In *Disc & Music Echo* in January 1971, she described what the two years of being in *Hair* meant to her:

The first year was tremendous and the first night was really exciting, as we didn't have any idea whether it would be a success or not. During the second year, I became disillusioned because the play was no longer what it was intended to be. It was supposed to be anti-establishment, but it became establishment itself.

In the early 1970s, it wasn't common for rock acts, or indeed progressive rock acts, to have female lead singers – or any female musicians for that matter. Renaissance with Annie Haslam springs to mind, but the two bands were very different stylistically. That said, the Curved Air song, 'Not Quite The Same', seems to have a few Renaissance-esque moments in terms of its rhythm and classical orchestration (of course, representing women in rock at the time was Suzi Quatro, as well as the bands Bertha and Fanny, but the fact is that such representation was arguably even less common in progressive rock). Sonja Kristina has been the one and only constant member of Curved Air. She told *Prog* in February 2018:

> Buffy Sainte-Marie was the first singer who wowed me. I learned several of her songs and would perform them at folk clubs alongside my own. I also loved Sandy Denny. What both of them have in common was being powerful and passionate, which was different to many other twee female singers back then.

The *Daily Mirror* reported in May 1973: 'Sonja Kristina, the twenty-four-year-old singer with the otherwise male group, Curved Air, reckons it's very hard for women to be taken seriously in the music business'. In the feature, Sonja said:

> You need a lot of dedication and stability. Girls can be as good musicians as men. They've got ten fingers, haven't they? The fact that rock is aggressive and outgoing doesn't mean that it's not feminine. Just you wait and see. There may only be a few of us now, but the next generation will see women accepted automatically as rock singers.

With regards to her experience of being the only woman in Curved Air, Sonja Kristina told *Prog* in February 2018:

> That never bothered me – or them for that matter. We had no inhibitions. I was very comfortable getting undressed in front of them. It wasn't that I was one of the boys, but more that we accepted each other and could therefore be fully open.

As soon as the UK production of *Hair* had finished, Curved Air launched a UK tour that was well-received, and that summer, they signed a record deal with Warner Bros. They were the first British band on the company's books. Warner Bros. hadn't been the only label who wanted to sign

Curved Air. With PR man, Tony Brainsby, stirring up excitement for the band, a bidding war saw Warner Bros. emerge as the winners, but to the tune of £100,000. Such was the extent to which Curved Air were in demand as a new band. Sonja Kristina explained in *Record Collector* in April 2012:

> We were quite at ease with each other. What excited me most was that they had strong, dramatic material composed already, though they didn't have much in the way of lyrics. As 1970 got underway, we were at the heart of a bidding war, but we'd earned the attention, having been on the club and university circuit for about six months, travelling in a coach with a broken heating system, sleeping in it or in communes. We built up grass-roots support – 'Vivaldi' always got a standing ovation – and the press picked up on us before the release of the first album, which was recorded through a publishing deal with Island before Warners contracted us for an enormous advance. When *Air Conditioning* came out, we toured with Black Sabbath – an unlikely coupling, but a successful one. I fell in love with Malcolm Ross, their personal manager, who I married.

It was reported in the *Daily Mirror* in October 1971: 'Sonja Kristina, twenty-two, lead singer with Curved Air, secretly married her manager Mal Ross at a little church in Marylebone on October 11'.

Curved Air's first album, *Air Conditioning*, was released in November 1970. It was a ground-breaking recording that was lavishly issued as rock's first-ever picture disc. Offering a healthy balance of ambitious hard rockers and strongly classically-influenced songs, the album got to number eight in the UK chart, and while the accompanying single, 'It Happened Today', didn't get much attention, Curved Air still began 1971 on the very edge of superstardom. After just one album, they were about to make some very memorable waves throughout the majority of the decade.

Second Album saw Ian Eyre replace Rob Martin on bass, and the new group line-up made their mark in the summer of 1971 when 'Back Street Luv' shot to number 4 in the charts. It did so ahead of *Second Album*'s release. The album itself was perhaps considered by some as somewhat of a lesser achievement than its predecessor, as it climbed no higher than number eleven in the charts.

In spring 1972, Curved Air released their acclaimed album, *Phantasmagoria*. Memorable tracks include 'Marie Antoinette' and the album's title track. *Phantasmagoria* got to number 20. Also, a song not on the LP, 'Sarah's Concern', was released as a single, but went by largely unnoticed.

Curved Air were enjoying much success on tour, but the stress of things was such that they split up for what would not be the last time. Darryl Way formed a new band, Wolf. Pilkington-Miksa joined Kiki Dee's band, and Monkman moved into session work. Sonja Kristina kept the Curved Air name, and she and bassist Mike Wedgwood (who replaced Ian Eyre for *Phantasmagoria*) brought in an entirely new line-up: Jim Russell (drums), Kirby Gregory (guitar), and Eddie Jobson (violin and synthesizers). With this line-up, Curved Air released the album *Air Cut* in 1973. It was considered by some to be very much a last attempt at making a go of things. Although the line-up did begin to record a second album – *Lovechild* – it was shelved when Curved Air broke up that summer. Jobson swiftly resurfaced as Brian Eno's replacement in Roxy Music. Mike Wedgwood joined Caravan. *Lovechild* would not see the light of day until it was released years later in 1990.

Not long after Curved Air had first broken up, Sonja Kristina initially had intentions of launching a solo career. However, in the autumn of 1974, the original band line-up reunited for what they had planned to be a one-off British tour. The line-up of Kristina, Way, Monkman, and Pilkington-Miksa was completed by bassist Phil Kohn. By performing the songs that many fans were most into, the group managed to touch upon what it was that had captured people's imaginations in the first place. This resulted in the release of the *Curved Air Live* album. The rejuvenation, however, was not such that it managed to keep the line-up united, and when Curved Air again resurfaced, in autumn 1975, Kristina and Way remained, having recruited new musicians; guitarist, Mick Jacques; bassist, John Perry; keyboardist, Pete Woods and drummer, Stewart Copeland. (Perry would be replaced by Greenslade's Tony Reeves in 1976).

The two albums released in 1975 and 1976 – *Midnight Wire* and *Airborne* respectively – were both met with a mixed reception. Stylistically, they were different from Curved Air's earlier albums. Inevitable, really, considering the line-up changes. Darryl Way was the first to leave, following one final unsuccessful single – an upbeat version of 'Baby Please Don't Go'. New musicians continued to join Curved Air (Alex Richman from Butts Band), but the group lasted only a few more months before splitting in late 1976. Copeland promptly joined The Police, Reeves re-formed Greenslade, and Kristina launched her solo career.

Curved Air are a fascinating band because across all the different line-ups spanning from 1970 to 1976, there were so many talented musicians putting their innovative ideas and skills into the music. As a result of this, it would probably be very easy to view Curved Air as a briefly-existing musical institution with a revolving door. The complexities of who was in the band and when is such that it makes for a rock family tree that would make quite a diagram. I can see why this might put people off engaging with a band. Throughout this book, I will do everything possible to get across the talent thatcomes across on each of Curved Air's albums. Commercially, they certainly had their ups and downs, but musically, each album offered something worthwhile, even if some were perhaps more memorable (and with more replay incentive) than others.

What follows is a brief biography of each member of Curved Air. It wouldn't be right to leave anyone out, but I have been unable to find biographic information on the following members, so I shall name them here in the interests of ensuring that everyone is credited: Ian Eyre, Rob Martin, Jim Russell, Mick Jacques and Phil Kohn.

When he was sixteen, Darryl Way won a scholarship to Dartington College of Arts to study violin. When he was eighteen, he turned down a scholarship to the Guildhall School of Music in favour of studying under Antonio Brosa at the Royal College of Music. Prior to being one of the founding members of Curved Air, Way's talents were already providing him with numerous prestigious opportunities. Brosa had been a pupil of nineteenth-century virtuoso violinist and composer Sarasate. After completing his education, Way joined forces with Francis Monkman: a prize-winning harpsichordist and organist from the Royal Academy of Music. During his time with Curved Air, Way was one of the writers of their hit, 'Back Street Luv'. He was a major contributor to the writing of three of the band's top-20 albums. Way explained in *Goldmine* in September 2018:

> I wanted a career as a violinist. My goal was to be second violin in a quartet, without the pressure of being first violin. I had changed schools, from being a big fish in a small pond at my prior school, to attending the Royal College of Music in London. It was daunting. Some of my classmates were practising eight hours a day. It was '67 and '68 London. I heard the bands Nice with Keith Emerson and Spooky Tooth with Gary

Wright and Mike Harrison, and I wanted to be part of that scene. I tried to figure out how my violin could be heard among that music. I went to the Orange shop on Denmark Street and put metal strings on my violin. I asked if they could amplify it. They succeeded doing that with a pick-up, and then I could play as loud as the rock electric guitars.

Other than Sonja Kristina, who has been on every Curved Air album, Darryl was the mainstay of the band. He appeared on all the band's 1970s albums with the exception of *Air Cut*. This was due to him briefly leaving the band at the end of 1972, when he cited musical differences and personality clashes as a contributing factor in his decision. In an interview with *Music Street Journal* in October 2013, Darryl Way stated who his influences were: 'As a violinist, David Oistrakh. Rock-wise – Spirit, King Crimson, Spooky Tooth and Family. As a composer – Prokofiev, Bartok and Puccini'.

Francis Monkman had a classical grounding in music, which certainly accounts for his very fluent keyboard technique, but he didn't quite complete his training due to the timing of other opportunities. He told *Electronics & Music Maker* in March 1983:

Curved Air started in about 1969 – that dove-tailed with the end of my studies at the Royal Academy of Music. I had to decide between the second half of my B.Mus and going on the road. It wasn't a very hard decision! The first keyboard I started using in Curved Air was a Hohner piano, but by the second album, I was using a VCS3 with the Cricklewood keyboard. The first album, *Air Conditioning*, also used the VCS3, but just for a few sweeps and effects, including a crazy violin solo through a ring modulator.

What comes across is that Monkman never stopped learning and never stopped experimenting. He may have left the Royal Academy of Music before completing his music degree, but that is certainly not to say that it put a stop to his development as an artist.

Florian Pilkington-Miksa was born in June 1950. He was the third of five brothers. His mother was English and his Polish father was a fighter pilot during the war. Florian was educated at Eton, but considering himself as not being particularly academic, he spent the majority of his time in the art department or playing drums. After his time at Eton, Florian went to Hammersmith Art School. This, however, didn't strike a chord with him in the way that he perhaps had hoped for. Influenced by his parents, he nearly joined the army. He was accepted by the regiment of the eleventh Hussar's, but whilst preparing for such commitment, he realised that it wasn't what he wanted to do.

Mike Wedgwood was born in 1950 in Derby. He joined The Overlanders in 1968 following their biggest hit – a cover of The Beatles' song, 'Michelle' – and remained with them until 1971. He is featured on their singles as The New Overlanders: 'Unchained Melody' and 'These Are Not My People'. After a stint with the band, Arthur's Mother, Wedgwood joined Curved Air in 1972. He played on *Phantasmagoria*. When the band split after making *Phantasmagoria*, Wedgewood stayed with Sonja Kristina and was active in helping to form a new band line-up. Wedgewood was active on *Air Cut* and *Lovechild* prior to Curved Air breaking up again in 1973.

When Kirby Gregory first played the guitar, he fell in love with it. In his late teens, he moved to London and joined Armada: a jazz-rock band featuring the jazz legend Sammy Rimmington. Two years later, Gregory joined Curved Air, where he was active on the albums *Air Cut* and (the unreleased at the time) *Lovechild*, as well as touring with them. As was reported in *Beat Instrumental* in December 1972:

Kirby Gregory started to teach himself to play the guitar when he was ten, by listening to numbers by The Beatles and The Stones. At fourteen he moved from Reading to Weston-Super-Mare, where he became part of various local pop and blues groups. At sixteen he left school and joined a band called Maya, which he brought up to London. The following year, he split and joined Armada. After a while, Armada began leaving him, and finally he was the only member left. At that point, he met up with Elmer Gantry, and together they formed another group under the same name. Even this fell apart, and in the end he sought refuge in session work. It was during this period that he received the phone call from Sonja Kristina.

Eddie Jobson joined Curved Air in 1973 at the age of just seventeen. His role in the band was to fill the violin vacancy Darryl Way had left, as well as filling Francis Monkman's shoes on keyboards: a daunting task by any stretch of the imagination. Prior to Curved Air, Jobson had been in a band called Fat Grapple, where he had played at some of the same venues as Curved Air. He appeared on *Air Cut* and *Lovechild*. Jobson made a significant contribution to the extraordinary piece, 'Metamorphosis' on

Air Cut. He also co-wrote 'Armin'. He was also instrumental on 'Joan' and 'Paris By Night' on *Lovechild*.

Tony Reeves began playing the orchestral double bass as a teenager. He played in local jazz-oriented groups with his Lewisham school friends. Reeves began his professional music career in 1964. He was a founding member of The Wes Minster Five. He played on their only two releases: both 1964 singles, 'Shakin' The Blues' and 'Sticks And Stones'. In 1968, he was invited to play bass with John Mayall's Bluesbreakers on the *Bare Wires* album. Reeves then co-founded Colosseum in 1970, playing on their first three albums before leaving for session work. His career as a session musician has included playing and producing for many artists: The Woods Band, Sandy Denny, Paul Kent, John Martyn, Days Of The Phoenix and Chris DeBurgh. In 1972 he joined his friend and Colosseum member, Dave Greenslade, in Greenslade's own eponymous band and stayed through 1974. Reeves worked with Curved Air towards the end of the band's tenure in the 1970s.

Alex Richman is from New York. A keyboardist and vocalist, her first band was called St John. They were the opening act for artists such as The Allman Brothers and Rufus in Chicago and Zephyr and Flash Cadillac in Boulder, Colorado. Richman recorded an album for Capitol Records featuring Ry Cooder on guitar, toured with Danny O'Keefe, performed and recorded with The Brothers Johnson, Ray Parker Jr. and Butts Band featuring Robbie Krieger and John Densmore of The Doors. When Richman toured with Curved Air in 1976, she was to be the last new recruit before they broke up and remained dormant for the rest of the decade.

Stewart Armstrong Copeland was born in Alexandria, Virginia, in 1952. He was the youngest of four children of Alabama-born CIA officer Miles Copeland Jr., and Scottish archaeologist Lorraine Adie. The family moved to Cairo, Egypt, not long after Stewart was born. He spent his formative years in the Middle East. In 1957, his family moved to Beirut, Lebanon, and Copeland attended the American Community School there. He began taking drum lessons when he was twelve and, within a year, was playing drums for school dances. Later he moved to England, where from 1967 to 1969, he attended Millfield, Britain's most expensive public school at the time. Copeland went to college in California, where he attended the United States International University and the University of California, Berkeley. Upon his return to England, he worked as road manager for Curved Air's 1974 reunion tour. It was during 1975 and 1976 that he would contribute to the band as their drummer. When Copeland's father realised that his son was serious about learning the drums, he insisted that he take proper tuition. Copeland told the *Daily Express* in May 2014:

> I had a classical musical education but never used it in my rock 'n' roll days. The easiest way to scare a rock musician is to hold a sheet with dots on the page in front him.

It was after studying at college in California that Stewart Copeland returned to Britain, and then joined Curved Air.

Sonja Kristina Linwood (as she was credited on Curved Air's debut album, *Air Conditioning*) is the granddaughter of acclaimed Swedish actress Gerda Lundequist. Sonja Kristina first got noticed when playing the role of Crissy in the original West End production of *Hair* in 1968. It was around this time that she was also involved with the running of the famous Troubadour Club in west London, which was a haven for folk musicians. Sonja Kristina told *Record Collector* in April 2012:

> My mother had been brought up by a famous Scandinavian actress, Gerda Lundequist, who was known as the Swedish Sarah Bernhardt. My father was the headmaster of a boy's borstal. Not many of my friends' parents wanted them to drop 'round our place, so I had quite a solitary childhood. I discovered drama when I was at a girls' convent school in Brentwood, where my big moment was playing Shylock in *The Merchant Of Venice*. I also passed grade exams – reciting poetry and prose, learning how to create a spell with words. I took Spanish guitar lessons at school, but I taught myself mostly from a book called *101 American Folk Songs*. A friend and I used to play and sing in harmony during assemblies. My vocal range wasn't always comfortable in the prescribed keys, so I had to learn to transpose things. I enjoyed the adrenaline rush of performing and, from the age of thirteen, was playing floor spots in folk clubs 'round Romford and Brentwood. As well as Buffy Sainte-Marie, my repertoire centred on the likes of Tom Paxton, Phil Ochs, Donovan and The Incredible String Band, and I began writing my own stuff. When I was fifteen, I contacted Roy Guest, the top manager for folk artists at the time, who was to run NEMS for a while. He managed The Piccadilly Line, who eventually became Edward's Hand. They had an album on CBS, called *The Huge World Of Emily Small*. I did tracks from it with them for an engagement at The Marquee. Roy got me on folk festivals

and television, including a spot on *Something's Coming* – a BBC series on which I sang my own songs, none of which I have recorded. I think they would sound very naïve now. I also ran a psychedelic club night at The Troubadour in Earl's Court on Wednesday evenings in 1967 when I was at college.

Sonja Kristina told in *Prog* in February 2018:

I was nineteen when I ran my own night at the club. But I did it through serendipity and intuition rather than hard business acumen. For instance, one day I ended up chatting to someone on the tube and it turned out he did lights. So I got him along to do the lights at The Troubadour. I'd meet poets and folk musicians and ask them to come down and perform. That was the way it all happened. I also had good friends like Al Stewart appearing. Overall it was a very successful time, but I was deeply in love with the hippieness of it all, rather than learning about the music business. I did a few shows with Piccadilly Line, who went on to change their name to Edward's Hand. We even got to do a gig at The Marquee Club in London – that was a highlight. They had some really nice songs.

In the same feature, Sonja Kristina recalled her earliest music memories:

At school, I used to do songs like 'My Grandfather's Clock', accompanying myself on guitar. That was to assembly gatherings. I also did proper concerts at the local boys' school! When I was trying to learn a tune a day, my dad would give me a shilling for everyone I succeeded with. That was his idea, not mine. My mum would sit and listen to me reciting poetry and extracts from Shakespeare when I needed to do that for any exams. My mother was talented enough to have gone on stage if she'd wanted. I have tapes of her singing, which were done from very scratchy recordings. And my dad was once an amateur puppeteer.

Prior to getting the role as Crissy in *Hair*, Sonja Kristina had numerous career opportunities and successes. As a result of the song that she performed on the television programme, *Something's Coming*, she got several letters and an offer to do a schools television series. It was around this time that Sonja met Al Stewart. She spent a year at the New College of Speech and Drama in Hampstead, and her time at college broadened her whole scope and taught her the basics of stage dynamics. There followed

a period of singing on the street, in tube stations and outside London's Middle Earth club in Covent Garden – the birthplace of the British progressive music scene. It was through this network that she got a job as vocalist with the blues band, The Piccadilly Line, who were resident at The Marquee. Sonja took over the running of a Wednesday night mixed-media show at The Troubadour Club in Earl's Court. There she met many people connected with the business, not the least of whom was Dave Cousins of Strawbs fame, who is rumoured to have considered her as a replacement for Sandy Denny. It was not to be, however, and after another period of barefooting it around London (at the time of the whole hippie/flower power thing), Sonja auditioned for the *Hair* musical, which was due to open in London. Initially, she was just to be part of the tribe, but her singing at rehearsals impressed the producer to the extent that Sonja was cast in the major role of Crissy.

It was in 1969 that Sonja Kristina was introduced to the band that would ultimately come to be known as Curved Air. Throughout the 1970s and beyond, she was instrumental in establishing the band as one of the most creative and exciting on the progressive rock scene. Her stage presence and sultry voice was such that she was a key figure behind Curved Air's success, not only musically but also commercially.

1970

Air Conditioning (1970)

Personnel:

Sonja Kristina: lead vocals

Darryl Way: violin, backing vocals

Francis Monkman: guitars, keyboards

Rob Martin: bass

Florian Pilkington-Miksa: drums

Studio: Island Studios, London

Producer: Mark Edwards

Highest chart positions: UK: 8

Side one: 1. 'It Happened Today' (Francis Monkman, Sonja Kristina Linwood) 4:55, 2. 'Stretch' (Darryl Way, Monkman) 4:05, 3. 'Screw' (Way, Linwood) 4:03, 4. 'Blind Man' (Way, Rob Martin) 3:32, 5. 'Vivaldi' (Way) 7:26

Side two: 6. 'Hide And Seek' (Way, Linwood) 6:15, 7. 'Propositions' (Monkman) 3:04, 8. 'Rob One' (Martin) 3:22, 9. 'Situations' (Way, Martin) 6:17, 10. 'Vivaldi' (With Cannons) (Way, Monkman) 1:35

One other song was recorded and released only on singles:

'What Happens When You Blow Yourself Up' (Monkman, Linwood) 3:34

In *Beat Instrumental* in March 1971, Darryl Way surmised what 1970 meant for the band: 'In that year, we've gone through all the necessary stages to handle where we are now. Small gigs, bad gigs, parties and so on'.

Curved Air's debut album, *Air Conditioning*, was released at the end of 1970. It was quite the success. It got to number 8 in the UK charts and it includes one of the band's most iconic songs, Darryl Way's 'Vivaldi'. The combination of Sonja Kristina's distinctive vocals, Francis Monkman's instrumental keyboard prowess, and Darryl Way on violin, makes for some fascinating music.

It was (and perhaps still is) considered by some that the success of Curved Air's first album was largely based on a very clever and unique marketing technique used to draw attention to the record. The album was initially released as a picture disc. It may be the case that it was the first commercially-produced picture disc. If it wasn't the first, it was certainly one of the very earliest instances of such technology being embraced by a record company. So much so that with the technology being in its infancy, it may not have been the best choice for sound quality. Still, though, the album was designed to be visually desirable, and this is something that certainly could have helped to encourage sales, even if people may not have been familiar with the music on the disc. The *Thanet Times* reported in November 1970:

A technique which originated in Germany has prompted a new British group to revolutionise LP sleeves. The eye-popping designs printed in bright colours practically leap out at you from the record itself. Curved Air are the group who have latched on to the German born idea of printing designs on a covering of art paper which is pressed on both sides of the disc and then covered with a coating of plastic. Then the grooves which produce the music are pressed on top of the plastic. Dust prone? Curved Air's record company, Warner Records, have surmounted that problem by slipping the album into a see-through jacket.

The hype generated around *Air Conditioning* meant that it found an audience far quicker than it otherwise may have done, but importantly, that is not to say that as the band's first album, it was without musical merit (far from it!). The album is very much a collaborative effort whereby all members of Curved Air contributed material. The opening track, 'It Happened Today', is a distinctive song that features some skilled solos and a classically-influenced coda. It features strong vocals, backed by some excellent violin, particularly on the slower instrumental ending. In contrast, the second track, 'Stretch', opens with violin before morphing into something of a glam-rock-style anthem. 'Screw' carries the album along nicely onto 'Blind Man', which is largely acoustic. This track really showcases the beauty of Sonja Kristina's vocals. The energetic 'Vivaldi' is such an iconic element of *Air Conditioning*. 'Hide And Seek' showcases Francis Monkman's guitar talents. The following track, 'Propositions' – with its intelligently layered guitars – continues to show Monkman's talents in a favourable light. A short track, it has some enjoyable dual guitar-playing and has a psychedelic feel to it – the type of track that would lend itself well to live instrumental jamming. The calm instrumental, 'Rob One', comes before the intricate track, 'Situations', which features another exuberant guitar solo. A reprise of 'Vivaldi' closes the album on a dramatic note.

The softer tracks – 'Screw' and 'Situations' – function as an excellent vehicle for Sonja Kristina to bring her unique voice to the fore. Her versatility is evident on the funkier and more upbeat tracks, 'Stretch' and 'Hide And Seek'. The two 'Vivaldi' tracks could be regarded as signature pieces of the album. 'Vivaldi' is a seven-minute track featuring virtuoso multi-tracked electric violin. While loosely-influenced by the work of the namesake composer, it is ultimately an original composition (it was later covered on keyboards by Francis Monkman in Sky). The theme is reprised at a somewhat more sedate pace, but with exploding firework sounds on the shorter, 'Vivaldi With Cannons', closing the *Air Conditioning* album.

Although Sonja Kristina is solely credited for the lyrics of 'It Happened Today', during various interviews that took place in the late 1990s, Francis Monkman asserted that he conceived the song's title and concept. Sonja corroborated that Monkman came up with the title. Sonja was quoted in Chris Welch's liner notes for the 2011 release of *Air Conditioning*, advocating that the lyrics to 'It Happened Today' are not 'really about anything specific'. 'Propositions' is credited entirely to Monkman. The Terry Riley influence is certainly noticeable in the song's high-energy rock, as it goes into a tape-loop-like improvisation. Both the music and lyrics for 'Situations' were written jointly by Darryl Way and Rob Martin. Martin recalled that when writing together, their rapport was such that they would bounce off each other, to the extent that very often each melody was produced alternately by first one composer, then the other. The lyrics of 'Hide And Seek' describe a post-apocalyptic scenario in which a lone survivor searches in vain for another living person. Sonja Kristina has stated that this lyric can be taken literally or symbolically. She quoted in the 2011 *Air Conditioning* liner notes: 'It's a nightmare, the sort of thing when you dream about being left in an empty city'. In the same liner notes, it is advocated that Sonja Kristina's vocals on 'Blind Man' were inspired by Donovan's performance on his song, 'Hurdy Gurdy Man'.

As much as some criticised *Air Conditioning* for being hyped in the way it was marketed, musically it is an ambitious and exciting album that, arguably, deserved its place in the top 10. The use of electric violin – as featured on 'Vivaldi' and 'Stretch' – is loud, driving and certainly attention-grabbing. The album did well and tours of small venues in the UK seem to have paid off for Curved Air as a new band at the time. The *Aberdeen Evening Express* reported on 2 December 1970:

Despite the poor turnout at the Fleetwood Mac concert bill two weeks ago, south promoters still haven't lost faith in the city as a crowd-pulling venue, and a top progressive package has been announced for

January. Coming forth for a Music Hall concert under the aegis of the Chrysalis Agency on January 16 are highly-quoted new group, Curved Air, plus Black Sabbath and Freedom. Reports from the south say that Curved Air have a highly individual style, with the violin the dominant solo instrument. Their debut album, Air Conditioning, has already sold 20,000 copies, which isn't bad going. Black Sabbath, of course, still have Paranoid in the top thirty. The following week we have Deep Purple, Ashton, Gardner and Dyke in concert, and then Elton John.

When asked to describe his biggest Spinal Tap moment, Darryl Way told *Music Street Journal* in October 2013: 'Something that involves Ozzy Osbourne that is not repeatable'. Touring with Black Sabbath must have been a fun experience.

In *Hit Channel* in December 2018, Sonja Kristina recalled what it was like being on tour with Black Sabbath:

They were very crazy guys. They were all naughty boys. They broke eggs on their manager's car, they used to throw things out of the window as they were driving along the motorway and they would put things in drinks. I started a relationship with their tour manager (Malcolm Ross) and then we got to get married – after a while – but when we went to the hotel room with Mal, they were sending us the room service late at night, hanging condoms full of water at the door for us, these kinds of things. Funnily enough, I had very long chats with Geezer Butler and Tony Iommi about black magic and spiritual things, because that subject matter was initially behind their performance and their material and all that vibration. It was so interesting that we were opening up the show for them. Because our music was so different, but the audience really liked what we did and it was good to feel that we matched Black Sabbath with our energy and power, and that the audience were transported to other levels than a round of devils.

Line-up changes were, generally speaking, a constant feature of Curved Air's tenure throughout the 1970s. In April 1970, Rob Martin was replaced by Ian Eyre on bass. *Air Conditioning* was recorded in July 1970 and was released in November.

The compromised sound quality on the original picture disc LP is undeniable. It is somewhat muffled and lacks clarity in places. With picture disc technology being in its infancy at the time, the sound quality of Curved Air's output was understandably scaled down. Still, by overlooking the technical limitations of the album's original release, what stands out in the grand scheme of things is an enjoyable landmark album that ultimately stood to launch Curved Air's career. As a journalist, Phil Symes, reported in *Disc & Music Echo* in January 1971: '(Sonja Kristina) was somewhat surprised by the immediate success of the first album but doesn't think it was due to the multi-coloured plastic disc. She says that, if anything, the gimmick hindered the album'.

In the same feature, Sonja Kristina advocated:

> People think of anything like that as hype. If a group have a hit with its own original material, then it's not a bad thing. It's bad that people look down on a best-selling single. Selling out only applies if a group goes out of its way to be commercial, which we won't be doing.

It is difficult to describe *Air Conditioning* as anything other than very good music. It is a bias that fans of the band are likely to hold, but essentially, it is the album that propelled Curved Air into the musical career that would span the 1970s and beyond; a career that included many gigs with high profile bands, and further album successes that went beyond the more eccentric marketing strategies used for *Air Conditioning*.

There is a sense that throughout their tenure, Curved Air were one of those bands that people either loved or hated, with little in between. A number of reviews related to *Air Conditioning* are reflective of that. Some of the complaints are about how the band was marketed and some are about the music itself. In January 1971, the *Daily Mirror* simply described the single, 'It Happened Today', as being a 'near miss from Curved Air'. But the single was given some positive attention when reviewed by *Record Mirror* in February 1971:

> With the hit album, the acres of publicity space and umpteen other features, this should score heavily. It is a very good value-for-money single, with Sonja doing her own occasionally imperturbable thing – and in the same inventive edginess in the backing. Good group this, a bargain single, actually.

The *Coventry Evening Telegraph* complained of the album in December 1970:

The gimmicks this week come from Curved Air. The music on *Air Conditioning* is falsely straining after a goal it never reaches. And the record itself has been produced in a revolutionary new process, so that information which normally appears on the sleeve is printed beneath a transparent playing surface.

Also, *Air Conditioning* didn't go unnoticed in the US. As with the UK, the album was met with a level of scepticism due to the way it had been marketed. *Air Conditioning* was reviewed in *Cash Box* in February 1971:

Curved Air, latest of Great Britain's hype groups, more than live up to the advance publicity. Sonja Kristina supplies deep-throated husky vocals that duel with Darryl Way's drifting electric violin. Sonja also provides interesting lyrics to melodies composed by the group's Way, Francis Monkman, and Robert Martin. Monkman, in particular, excels in his lead guitar and keyboard work. The latter, especially, encompasses a wide variety of instruments, ranging from organ to piano to Mellotron to harpsichord to synthesizer. All in all, an auspicious debut, marred only by some, at times, rather pedestrian drumming.

What is particularly striking about Curved Air, though, is the fact that people who liked them 'really' liked them. In December 1970, the *Buckinghamshire Examiner* focussed more on the music itself than how it had been marketed, and positively so:

Air Conditioning is a beautiful record. The credits and track titles are all inscribed on the disc and there is no cover. The band rely on electric violinist Darryl Way for much of their innovation. Lovely classical pieces and folk-rock swell to an incredible fusion. Sonja Kristina's voice spills like wine and tumbles between the instrumentation. Francis Monkman plays lead guitar, organ, piano, Mellotron, electric harpsichord, special effects equipment and VCS3 synthesizer. Robert Martin plays bass and Florian Pilkington-Miksa plays drums. A fabulous album.

Curved Air recorded a *Christmas Carol Concert* for John Peel's *Top Gear* show, with Marc Bolan, Robert Wyatt, Mike Ratledge and Faces in December 1970. Sonja Kristina reminisced in *Hit Channel* in December 2018:

It was fantastic to be in the same room with all those wonderful people. Rod Stewart sang a beautiful version of 'Away In A Manger' because it was so moving. I've got a recording of the concert.

1971

Second Album

Personnel:
Sonja Kristina: lead vocals
Darryl Way: violin, backing vocals, piano (5)
Francis Monkman: guitars, keyboards, VCS3 synthesizer
Ian Eyre: bass guitar
Florian Pilkington-Miksa: drums
Peter Zinovieff: electronics 'by courtesy of'
Engineer: Colin Caldwell
Album design: John Kosh
Studios: Island Studios and Morgan Studios, London
Producers: Colin Caldwell and Curved Air
Highest chart places: UK: 11
Side One. 1. 'Young Mother' (Darryl Way, Sonja Kristina Linwood) 5:55, 2. 'Back Street Luv' (Way, Linwood, Ian Eyre) 3:38, 3. 'Jumbo' (Way, Linwood) 4:11, 4. 'You Know' (Way, Linwood) 4:11, 5. 'Puppets' (Way, Linwood) 5:26
Side Two. 6. 'Everdance' (Francis Monkman) 3:08, 7. 'Bright Summer's Day '68' (Monkman) 2:54, 8. 'Piece Of Mind' (Monkman) 12:52

Sonja Kristina considered in *Disc & Music Echo* in January 1971:

I don't really know how successful we are or how long we'll continue to be successful. What I get very frightened about is the thought of getting near the top and then falling. I just wonder if we're happening at the right time and whether we're ready for it. I think we probably are.

She told *Disc* in April 1972:

There are such dangers in becoming an overnight success. People are asking you what your secret is. And you have no idea; you went on stage and did your best and went down well. The second awful stage is when people say, 'Ha ha, and what are you going to do now?', and part of you wants to keep that success going, so you think, 'What was it we did?', and that affects you. We were so inexperienced before – now we're experienced, we have some foundation. We didn't want to be a formula band, though, so the second album was almost deliberately not like the first one, and people were saying, 'There isn't another 'Vivaldi'. We wanted our public to see us developing in the way that we were going and that they would come with us – we hoped it would be one hundred per cent, but it didn't matter that much.

Darryl Way said of 'Vivaldi' in *Beat Instrumental* in March 1971:

It's very difficult to beat it for excitement. You can either write something faster or louder, but it has to be completely different, and it's hard to write something more effective. We're putting in a middle section on the next album that we do on stage but which isn't on the first album. There's also some material that has developed out of material on the first album. The new album is really a clarification of the style of the group. I think the music has a lot more depth and we have got a lot more experience. The band has developed a lot from the time when the first album was recorded.

Still though, normal artist's anxiety aside, 1971 started off well for Curved Air. They were still touring on the back of *Air Conditioning*. Journalist, Howard Fielding, reviewed a gig that took place at the Town Hall in Birmingham, in *The Birmingham Post* in January 1971:

There was a rare value at last night's concert at the Town Hall with three groups performing – Freedom, Curved Air and Black Sabbath – and an enthusiastic audience exhausted itself clapping, shouting and dancing, especially to the two groups specialising in loud pulsating music: Freedom and Black Sabbath. Black Sabbath topped the bill and were far superior of the two, playing numbers from their last two LPs and some from their next. These particularly were hard, driving songs confirming that Sabbath is hoping to take over Led Zeppelin's role as champions of heavy music. 'Paranoid', 'Lucifer' and 'Into The Void' were their best songs. Quite the reverse happened for Curved Air, who were starting their first concert tour. The reputation of Darryl Way (electric violin), Francis Monkman (lead guitar and synthesizer) and Sonja Kristina (vocals) had preceded them, and they justified them fully by some brilliant individual performances.

The *Aberdeen Evening Express* reported in January 1971:

Aberdeen's pop concert programme for 1971 swings into action on Saturday night with an attractive three-group package bill from the

Chrysalis agency, featuring Black Sabbath, Curved Air and Freedom. Both Black Sabbath and Curved Air currently have albums in the top 30 LPs chart, at number 16 and number 18, respectively. Black Sabbath – who have just returned from a mammoth USA tour which includes three encores at Fillmore East – comprise Ozzy Osbourne (vocals), Geezer Butler (bass guitar), Tony Iommi (lead guitar) and Bill Ward (drums). The group, who have been compared to Led Zeppelin, have had two hit albums, *Black Sabbath* and *Paranoid*, which has led the group to declare that there will be no more singles issued. Curved Air have built up a considerable reputation on the strength of their debut album, *Air Conditioning*, which shot straight into the charts, complete with the sleeve design printed on the actual album. The group have been together nine months, and their music is described as a fusion of classical and rock with a warm female lead vocal sound. The violin is the dominating solo instrument. Says the delectable Sonja, an ex-*Hair* girl: 'Our music is a combination of the different tastes and individuality and influences of every member. Once we have an idea, we try to get that across in a precise way, still keeping that basic feeling'. They have a four-number maxi-single coming out on January 21, but first, they face a discerning Aberdeen audience – a large one, I hope.

Whilst not wishing to insinuate that one group is of a higher musical status than the other, I would advocate that Curved Air had achieved something very noteworthy in how, as a relatively new band, they were on the bill with a Black Sabbath who had certainly made a considerable dent in the journey of their career by then. In June 1971 in *The Birmingham Post*, journalist, Ian Rufus, reviewed a concert that took place at the Town Hall:

I don't normally hold with standing ovations at pop concerts. It is always so easy to mistake noise and exciting movement for well-performed music. Curved Air is different. The group deserved every clap, every whistle, and every stamped foot. Curved Air is a tremendously difficult band to classify, although it's certain that any classification would not go down well with the four men and girl who make up the group. Their musical ability is beyond question. They can all play their appointed instruments so well, in fact, that there need be no attempt to cover up with wild solos which swoop off at a tangent from the main theme. They have become masters with that strangest of instruments, the Moog synthesizer: an electronic, computer-like gadget which conjures up the weirdest solar sounds from nowhere at all. During 'Vivaldi' – Curved Air's musical *coup de grace* – they virtually left it to play itself, an awe-inspiring experience that I don't want to go through again in a hurry, but that I wouldn't have missed for the world. Curved Air is a credit to today's pop scene. It is almost too original for words.

The appropriately named *Second Album* was released in September 1971. The album got to number 11 in the charts in October 1971 and included their sole charting single, 'Back Street Luv', which got to number four in the UK charts in August 1971, prior to *Second Album* actually being released. It was after having recorded the album that the band signed with Clifford Davis Management.

The album cover included the image of a rainbow, in homage to Terry Riley's, *A Rainbow In Curved Air* album from which the band had taken their name. The content and arrangement of the material on *Second Album* is suggestive of the divisions that were cropping up in the band that would lead to their break-up the following year. All the songs on side one were composed by Darryl Way (with some assistance from Ian Eyre) with lyrics by Sonja Kristina, whilst all the songs on side two were composed by Francis Monkman. Splitting their individual work across each side of the record was seemingly demonstrative of the fact that Way and Monkman didn't co-write any of the material on *Second Album*. It is particularly striking because they did co-write tracks on *Air Conditioning*. Such division perhaps makes the order of the songs on *Second Album* present as being somewhat lumped together, but on balance, the song order is certainly not starkly inappropriate either, in terms of the overall flow of the album.

Second Album is certainly attention-grabbing as it opens with not one but two memorable songs: 'Young Mother', which includes an excellent instrumental break in its midst, and the iconic 'Back Street Luv'. In some ways, 'Young Mother' harks back to the pre-Curved Air days of Sisyphus, in its use of a swirling VCS3 synthesizer introduction that is almost on a loop as an orchestral fanfare between the horns and Darryl Way's violin. It creates an intense yet confrontational sequence. Sonja Kristina sings with emotion through the lyrical textures prior to Florian Pilkington-Miksa, Eyre, and the keyboards soaring through an almost space-age-sounding midsection. 'Jumbo' is demonstrative of a band stretching their wings in the intricately structured use of strings. 'You Know' is another good rocker that possibly hints at there being an influence from the American band Spirit, and it sounds a little bit like a nod to Procol Harum. It presents Monkman with the scope to channel the crunches of Robin Trower and Carlos Santana throughout the solo, with some bluesy work and riffing as the keyboards provide a steady foundation. Sonja and Darryl harmonise effectively together, keeping the music flowing and moving forward. 'Puppets' features fascinating use of hooks, and effective use of percussion, with Way's piano and Mellotron flowing through. 'Everdance' includes plenty of Curved Air trademark sounds in the prominent use of violin and an almost childlike nursery rhyme lyric that makes it easily memorable. The band interplay on 'Everdance' is a treat to hear, Darryl Way and Francis Monkman really seeming to bounce off of each other at times. Monkman's innovative approach is showcased on 'Bright Summer's Day 1968' in its use of quirky melodies and time signature changes. Closing off the second side of the LP is the elaborate 'Piece Of Mind', again a track where Monkman's singular music vision is strongly put across. This thoughtfully-structured suite offers lots of musical interest for the whole course of its thirteen minutes. 'Piece Of Mind' could be said to be a classical yet nightmarish-sounding theatrical composition. It's capped by a reading of T. S. Eliot's *The Wasteland*. Maybe that's what makes it sound so spooky. That said, the music itself certainly contributes towards that effect anyway. On the recital of T. S. Eliot's, *The Wasteland*, Sonja Kristina told *The Arts Desk* in April 2014:

> Francis stuck them in. 'Piece Of Mind' was entirely his own work. Like a great composer, he could just play a composition on a keyboard and know exactly who would play the different parts. That song is about being in a mental hospital. I think the Eliot lines just provide a bit of mood.

Not only was Francis Monkman instrumental in making Curved Air's music interesting thematically, he was also proactive in exploring a range of possibilities technically. Journalist, Michael Watts, reported in *Melody Maker* in September 1971:

> Although his band is very much a rock vehicle, Francis Monkman, the lead guitarist and keyboards musician with Curved Air, has been intently exploring the electronic possibilities during the past year. He has recently built an analogue computer (from a kit), whose basic function is as a

voltage control device for a synthesizer, and which in musical terms, therefore, changes the shape and pitch of a note. As far as he knows, one has never been used in a group before. Now he is working on the construction of a digital computer, a much more ambitious device, which will enable him to feed in a melody that can be played back at any speed in any form. At present, he's got as far as making the sequencer which controls the memory cores. In effect, when this is used on stage, it will be like having another member of the band, in that a solo on a conventional instrument can be transformed once it has entered the memory banks into a passage of sound totally different. Monkman has immersed himself totally in the whole subject of computers and their use in relationship to music. He has been to classes; he has read books on electronics, he has considered the effect of large scale adoption of computerised music on the nature of the rock business. Eventually, he believes, it will mean a complete break for a number of musicians from the commercial aspect of the present scene. At present, all groups, he thinks, are making compromises in their music purely so they can live. At some time, there will be a group that can devote themselves to something entirely divorced from showbiz while retaining certain rock aspects.

It would be easy to read the above and wonder if, as a musician, Monkman would have been concerned about doing himself out of a job. Fortunately, he saw the use of technology as an extension of what could be achieved musically rather than as a replacement for the human element of making music. In the same article, Monkman explained:

A computer can do nothing on its own without the human brain behind it. But then again, I don't see why it can't be programmed with what we term as emotion. It involves analysing what emotion is and projecting that into such and such a circumstance. Look at Terry Riley's work – how can you say that's devoid of emotionalism. When I first heard him, I thought I'd never want to listen to romanticism again. Here's something for once, that is free! To a musician, there are no barriers – or at least, there shouldn't be, despite where his main preferences lie. Those who do find barriers are up against themselves. For instance, I don't like Verdi and Italian opera because I can't accept their basic naivety, but I'm prepared to accept the fault is in myself. I can't understand it – there are music professors at the Academy (of Music) who can be incredibly knowledgeable about classical music but not know anything after 1930.

It just beats me how someone with a total insight into one kind of music can dismiss that on the other side. I think that the younger people discovering classical music are much more open-minded than the classical ones discovering rock.

Second Album was reviewed in the *Thanet Times* in October 1971:

To many fans, Curved Air are only familiar for their single, 'It Happened Today', and their high-riding 'Back Street Luv'. But to become air conditioned, it is necessary to hear the group's latest album. The *Second Album* is a conglomeration of ballad, rock, and catchy violin pieces. One track – the twelve-minute marathon 'Piece Of Mind' – has dirge-like tones. Here is a group with a veritable wealth of talent. Electric violinist Darryl Way, and Francis Monkman, have training in classical music, which marks them and their colleagues as a group ahead of their time. Then there's Sonja Kristina. You have heard her on 'Back Street Luv', which is also on *Second Album*. But there is also another side to her voice: Sonja, the wistful balladeer. Apart from 'Bright Summer's Day' and 'You Know', this side of her singing is evident on the album. And you wait with anticipation for her vocals on 'Young Mother' and 'Jumbo' with Darryl's classical violin pieces.

***Record Mirror* reviewed *Second Album* in the same month:**

More ambitious than the last album (musically, that is), Curved Air's style is more refined and definite on the second. There is an accent on strange and picturesque backings, such as the hollowness of 'Piece Of Mind'. It's a frantic album, very tense and anxious – almost unnerving. In opposition, what seems to be the best inclusion is a quiet, utterly uplifting track called 'Jumbo', which Sonja explains was written with a transatlantic flight in mind. The backing is absolutely incredible. Hear it. Also included is their hit, 'Back Street Luv'.

Unlike *Air Conditioning*, *Second Album* was recorded when most of the songs were freshly written and had had little time to be developed over the course of touring. An exception to this is the track, 'Young Mother', which began its life as a song by Way, Monkman and Pilkington-Miksa in Sisyphus. Then titled 'Young Mother In Style', it evolved into the form heard on *Second Album*, largely as a result of new lyrics by Sonja

Kristina. She told *Goldmine* in March 2018: 'Jackie Onassis was the inspiration for 'Young Mother', with a cry to be left alone and a theme of trying to be kind'.

In *Hit Channel* in December 2018, Sonja Kristina described how she worked with Darryl Way to write 'Young Mother':

> Darryl wrote the song, he performed it and he had lyrics: 'This young mother in style/Finds it hard to keep her smile'. When I was trying to sing those words, it didn't sit well with me, so I worked with the tune on my own and then came up with the new lyrics, which were based on how the melody and the movement of the song interacted with me. It's a big feeling and cry, a demand for respect, really.

Sonja Kristina said of 'Young Mother' in *The Arts Desk* in April 2014:

> It's just about being strong and kind, which was my philosophy of life at the time we originally recorded it and probably still is now. Darryl wrote it first. His original words were 'Young mother in style/Trying hard to keep her smile'. I just never settled into that version, so I got into the melody and stretched it and played the chords on the piano and sang over it. Then I came up with the words and the tune, and it moved me, which was great – so then it moved other people too.

The words originally penned by Darryl Way are actually on *Air Waves* (2012), the remastered BBC John Peel sessions.

Curved Air's progressive rock leanings on *Second Album* are evident on the epic track, 'Piece Of Mind'. Monkman considered the track to be his first attempt at composing something more extended; something that went beyond simple song structure. The song is reflective of the extent of musical complexity that Curved Air included in their shows around that time. 'Piece Of Mind' lends itself to lots of musical improvisation and creativity for a live performance. Sonja Kristina told *Hit Channel* in December 2018:

> A lot of the band's songs we did, had long improvisations, not only in 'Vivaldi', but compositions could be extended and any of the instrumental parts could be very free and it started to be part of the band, in a sense. This is what we did. I was so happy to get on stage and play free, which is exactly what I did with the musical *Hair*. We were

very free on stage, but there were parts that suddenly some of those were choreographed, so there would be set parts speaking and moving on stage and then you could go anywhere, and later you could come back to get to the same scene. Yes, we did a lot of improvisation.

It would seem that a somewhat academic approach to music probably went very much in Curved Air's favour as both writers and musicians. Journalist, Michael Watts, reported in *Melody Maker* in September 1971:

That rock is worth studying by academic minds he (Francis Monkman) accepts without question. There is an inevitability, he says, about the pattern of musical forms over the past century. The original need for rock music, particularly its accent on volume, he traces back to the early 1800s, when the overall noise level was so much lower than it is now, that to listen to a large orchestra created a tremendous physical experience (Beethoven's Seventh in 1830 would have been played as loud as a rock band plays now, he says by way of illustration). This volume level increased in classical music up until the time of Stravinsky and Varese in the 1920s, and by this period, jazz had achieved the position as the physical catalyst. With the post-war jazz people like Parker, however, Monkman believes that jazz lost its rhythmic feel so that by the fifties, the public was ready for a music which placed the accent almost totally on physical stress. And rock was there for that purpose. As rock in the sixties gradually became more intellectual in approach and content, though, the serious rock musician found himself placed with a problem: should he be writing rock and roll and be content to fulfil just that role? Or should he make use of new musical thinking, the new approaches to tonality, for example? At present, Monkman perpetuates that there are three categories of experimental musicians: the traditionalists, with whom Stockhausen has an affinity because of his romantic association with the Viennese School; the iconoclasts, like Cage and Cornelius Cardew, who is using non-musicians because he believes only they have freedom from preconceived notions; and the creators, among whom can be numbered Ligeti and Terry Riley, and possibly – because of his newest work – John Cage, who thus has a foot in both camps.

***Second Album* documents Curved Air at the peak of their popularity following the success of the single, 'Back Street Luv'. It is one of their**

best-known tracks (so much so that, unusually for a prog rock band perhaps, their song was covered by session musicians for the Volume 19 release of the *Top Of The Pops* LP on Hallmark Records). Curved Air released two versions of 'Back Street Luv'. The studio version was their iconic hit, and then four years later, they put out a live version. Their only appearance on *Top Of The Pops* was on 9 September 1971. Also performing on the show that week was Rod Stewart, Carole King, Shirley Bassey, The Fortunes and Marmalade. At the time of Curved Air's *Top Of The Pops* performance, 'Back Street Luv' was at number 9. A week later, it went up five places to its highest UK chart position of number 4. In August 1971, *Strathearn Herald* advocated of the single:

> 'Back Street Luv' gives a rather monotonous rhythm with vocals lacking drive. The B-side has more life to it but gets rather hairy in places. Rising up in the charts however, so there we are.

It would have been easy to feel daunted by the sudden success of 'Back Street Luv', but luckily, Sonja Kristina was a seasoned performer by then. In February 2018, she discussed the matter with *Prog*:

> We did *Top Of The Pops* and had a car sent for us. But I was used to this because I made TV appearances before on a folk music show, so was used to that sort of treatment. Being on a show like *Top Of The Pops* was fascinating because of the way the audience and the bands interacted. It was like watching natural history in action!

In *Record Collector* in April 2012, Sonja Kristina recalled the way in which Curved Air were welcomed in the States, all the more due to the success of 'Back Street Luv':

> We supported Jethro Tull, Deep Purple, Johnny Winter, Edgar Winter and B.B. King in huge stadiums. The second time we went over, however, the *Second Album* – the one we were promoting – didn't reach the shops until after we'd gone home. That was the one containing 'Jumbo' – about Darryl's homesickness while in the States – and 'Back Street Luv'. When that was a hit, the audiences reacted to our concerts with screaming!

Sonja Kristina told *Hit Channel* in December 2018:

It ('Back Street Luv') maybe was a little disturbing to release as a single because we hadn't released a single before, which was just like a kind of a showcase for the band. The first single was 'It Happened Today' with 'What Happens When You Blow Yourself Up' on the B-side. It's a very simple song with very simple lyrics that were very truthful and honest. As soon as I heard it played on the radio by DJ Alan Freeman, who played all the interesting charts music, it sounded really good, so I had a feeling then that it would do well. I was always very touched by the way people, all of a sudden, they identify with the song that we came up with, which is basically about skipping school and hanging out with undesirable older boys and men, just having a clandestine life. So maybe they don't know what it is about, but other people, obviously when they hear it, they interpret it in their own way, and I find that fascinating.

When asked about the inspiration for 'Back Street Luv', Sonja Kristina told Prog in March 2015:

When I was fifteen, I used to skip off school, and one day noticed a blond man standing on the steps at the local snooker hall. I became fascinated with him and ended up chasing and seducing him. He looked like a pop star, although I found out he'd been in prison and had a wife and child. But that didn't deter me from my interest in him and also some of his friends. However, I could never think about taking him home as my father ran a borstal, and this guy had once been an inmate there. So my dad would know who he was. I got found-out eventually and was suspended from my convent school. But the whole episode gave me the idea for the song.

Not bad going at all for a single that was actually rush-released! – as was reported in Record Mirror in June 1971 under the headline, 'Curved Air Rush Tour Single':

Curved Air, newly returned from their States tour, have written and are now rush-releasing a new single to coincide with the seventeen-date British itinerary, which now features a special Royal Festival Hall appearance. Titled 'Back Street Luv', the single was written immediately upon their return here and recorded for release on June 11. It was composed by Darryl Way, Sonja Kristina and Ian Eyre, and the flip side, 'Everdance', is a Francis Monkman composition.

Sonja Kristina told *Goldmine* in March 2018:

> Francis Monkman wrote the lyrics to 'Everdance', about the supernatural. The devil has all the best tunes. The inn is haunted and you have to dance until you die.

Musically, Curved Air were certainly a source of fascination for the media by 1971. It wasn't uncommon for their music to invite commentary on whether they were a rock group whose remit was to imbed classical music into their sound, or whether essentially, they were just doing what came naturally to them as a group of musicians with their respective training backgrounds and individual preferences. *The Liverpool Echo* reported under the title, 'Classical Strains In The Curved Air', in August 1971:

> It should come as no surprise if fans of the Curved Air group detect strains of classical music in their playing. Francis Monkman was about to take his degree in piano and harpsichord at the Royal Academy of Music when he decided to switch to self-taught guitar. Colleague, Darryl Way, studied violin for a year at the Royal College of Music, while drummer Florian Pilkington-Miksa, attended art college for a while after leaving Eton. Only bassist, Ian Eyre, graduated through the semi-professional rock band scene, although Sonja Kristina was a member of the cast of *Hair* before joining Curved Air as vocalist. The group, however, do not make a deliberate attempt to fuse classical and rock music together. Darryl and Francis insist that the classical influence involved in Curved Air's overall sound is original work written into the general context of the musical ideas they are trying to express. Since the recording of their first album last year, the group have put more emphasis on 'heavy' rock with a West Coast flavour, as heard on their new single, 'Back Street Luv' on the Warner Bros. label. On stage, Sonja sings with an energetic dash reminiscent of Janis Joplin, but the powerful delivery of lyrics is very much her own thing.

There was media interest in Sonja Kristina as Curved Air was becoming more well-known. The fact that she was a female singer, considered seductive by many, was likely to be a factor in this. In February 1971, the *Thanet Times* reported:

Curved Air's Sonja Kristina has the distinction of being the only female lead singer with any progressive group. And not surprisingly, she has been tipped as the female singer most likely to succeed in 1971. Curved Air are the group who are currently enjoying plenty of success with their *Air Conditioning* LP and the single record, 'It Happened Today'. Twenty-three-year-old Sonja – who is separated from her husband – divides her duties between the group and her two-year-old son, Sven. Clearly, a girl who likes to air her talents.

When Curved Air went into the studio to record *Second Album*, Rob Martin had to step down as a result of a trapped nerve in his shoulder; it made it impossible for him to play bass. An advert for a replacement was placed in *Melody Maker*. Enter one Ian Eyre. Eyre was from a Northern soul background; he played on tour with Curved Air and co-wrote 'Back Street Luv' with Sonja and Darryl. He is also present on *Live At The BBC*, which was released in 1995.

For any band, the second album is always a challenge; after the success of the first album, it is understandable that there is likely to be a level of pressure to live up to the same standards. It isn't uncommon for a second album to be recorded in the gaps of a busy touring schedule, with little time to come up with new material. In this regard, Curved Air were no exception. Still though, onwards and upwards. In *Beat Instrumental* in March 1971, Darryl Way described the solid perspex violin that was being made for him: 'A friend of mine is making it. It's going to sound beautiful, but it will be very heavy to play. It'll be nice to have everything perspex like the guitar and bass are already'. At the time, Way was still using an ordinary violin with steel strings that were amplified by a specially designed magnetic pick-up.

As a live band, the ball was certainly rolling, particularly by the end of spring, with stories and adverts for the 1971 Weeley Festival appearing in *Melody Maker* and other areas of the national music press. The bill included T. Rex, Status Quo and Rod Stewart. With no Isle of Wight Festival that year, Weeley stood out as a result. 150,000 people attended the festival.

Supported by the success in Britain of what essentially became their signature song - ` Back Street Luv' – a subsequent US tour followed. Curved Air's performance at the Fillmore East, New York, was reviewed in *Billboard* in May 1971:

Curved Air, probably one of the finest groups in the New York area, opened the first show at the Fillmore on May 1. Formed a little more than a year ago and recording on the Warner Brothers label, Curved Air began their set with 'It Happened Today'. This fast rock piece let Sonja Kristina, the female lead, belt out her message while a violin break containing classic overtones rounded out the songs. Sonja, and Darryl Way, the other vocalist, harmonised to 'Thinking On The Floor'. 'Propositions' and 'Vivaldi' were the best numbers, showing the sellout crowd a look into the future of electronic music.

'Thinking On The Floor' was never recorded in the studio, but a recording of it is available on the album released in 1995: *Live At The BBC*.

Disappointingly, Florian Pilkington-Miksa was sidelined by illness for a number of months. Although only in a temporary live capacity, Barry DeSouza was brought in to cover for him, a highlight being his appearance with Curved Air on German TV's *Beat Club*. Although Sonja's sultry appearance and vocals were perhaps the main focal point, Darryl Way's perspex electric violin provided something of a unique novelty in its appearance. Performing on the *Beat Club* TV show in Germany in 1971 was symptomatic of Curved Air's profile rapidly rising, and it opened up other opportunities for the band in Europe. Sonja Kristina told *Hit Channel* in December 2018:

> It was important. It was the second time we had played a big festival in Europe. It was the second rock gathering that we had played and we were building our audience there. The bands that were performing there were all exceptional and it was good to be on the same bill as all those. Also, when we finished the festival, we went on a dome just as we were packing up to go and they all gathered around us and stayed. It was a really magical moment and a very rapturous response.

Curved Air worked incredibly hard throughout 1971 and it was certainly all happening. Sonja Kristina was seemingly driven by a determination inspired by her home life. As was reported in *Disc & Music Echo* in January 1971:

> Sonja Kristina, the female element of Curved Air – the group predicted by many to be the one most likely to succeed in the coming year – is very content with her part in the group and happy about the success

of their first album *Air Conditioning*. But the most important thing in her life at present is her two-year-old son, Sven, and it's chiefly for his benefit she's working as hard as she is (she and her husband are now separated).

Sonja Kristina asserted in the same article:

I'm doing what I'm doing at the moment because I'm hung up on it. If it all fell through, I'd probably become a full-time mother … He's very important to me and I'm very much aware of him. I'm working as much as I can for him and for me. I'd like to ensure that he's alright materially and otherwise. I just want to be his mother. At the moment, he's living with my parents and I get to see him a lot, so things are alright. But I think when he's older, I will not want to work as hard, so he can be with me and I can help him. I don't want to be swamped by work, so that it gets me away from doing that. If I felt that was happening, I'd quit.

The journalist, Phil Symes, continued:

Money is only important to her because she says she needs it to support her son and to make sure her folks are alright. Curved Air is giving Kristina the opportunity to fulfil that responsibility, but that's not the only reason she's with the group. She's very much involved with the music, and for her, achieving her ambition and enjoying it. She says she has a lot of ambitions.

It must have been a very exciting time for Sonja Kristina. With Curved Air in the early stages of their journey, there was still much to learn, much to do and many other possibilities to dream about. Sonja Kristina told *Disc & Music Echo* in January 1971:

I have ambitions to do some weird things, like go on safari across the desert on a camel – it would probably be horrible, but I'd like to do it. I'd like to ride 'round Lapland on a horse. And I've always wanted to join a circus. But my ambition really is to master music, to make music flow through me, which it doesn't do. I want music to flow from my head into an instrument, or through my voice, without having to think too much because I really like music. You find out when you're doing something that it's something you've always wanted to do. I'm contented for now, but there's so much more to do. I'm learning all the time. Really I'm still in the process of learning a trade, so to speak.

1972

Phantasmagoria

Personnel:

Sonja Kristina: lead vocals, acoustic guitar (2)

Darryl Way: violin, keyboards (1, 3), tubular bells (1)

Francis Monkman: keyboards, electric guitar, percussion (8, 9)

Mike Wedgwood: bass, backing vocals, acoustic (6) and electric (9) guitar, percussion (9)

Florian Pilkington-Miksa: drums, percussion (9)

Guest musicians:

Annie Stewart: flute (2), Crispian Steele-Perkins: trumpet, Paul Cosh: trumpet, James Watson: trumpet, George Parnaby: trumpet, Chris Pyne: trombone, Alan Gout: trombone, David Purser: trombone, Steve Saunders: trombone, Frank Ricotti: xylophone, vibes, Mal Linwood-Ross: percussion, Colin Caldwell: percussion, Jean Akers: percussion, Doris the Cheetah: vocals (4)

Art direction: Richard Rockwood

Cover illustration: John Gorham

Studios: Advision Studios and E.M.S., London

Producers: Colin Caldwell and Curved Air

Highest chart places: UK: 20

Side One. 1. 'Marie Antoinette' (Darryl Way, Sonja Kristina Linwood) 6:20, 2. 'Melinda (More or Less)' (Linwood) 3:25, 3. Not Quite The Same (Way, Linwood) 3:44, 4. 'Cheetah' (Way) 3:33, 5. 'Ultra-Vivaldi' (Way, Francis Monkman) 2:22

Side Two 6. 'Phantasmagoria' (Monkman) 3:15, 7. 'Whose Shoulder Are You Looking Over Anyway?' (Monkman) 3:24, 8. 'Over And Above' (Monkman) 8:36, 9. 'Once a Ghost, Always A Ghost' (Monkman, Linwood) 4:25

One other track was recorded and released as a single, with 'Phantasmagoria' on the B-side: 'Sarah's Concern' (Way, Linwood) 3:20

It was reported in *Disc* in April 1972:

> Curved Air passed their second-anniversary last month and hopefully left their teething troubles behind them. By way of celebration, they have embarked on a mammoth and packed tour and released their new album, *Phantasmagoria*. Sonja Kristina married their personal

manager, Mal Ross, at the end of last year, and they share a flat with the group's violinist, Darryl Way, and keyboard and synthesizer player, Francis Monkman.

The band's rapport was such that they were indeed living together and seemingly happily so. All the members of the early-1970s line-up lived in a London flat together for a few years. When asked in an interview with *Prog* in February 2018 if it was a chaotic experience, Sonja Kristina explained:

No more chaotic than living with a family. Most of the time, we were kept busy rehearsing, touring or writing. We all had our own rooms at the flat, although Florian (Pilkington-Miksa) had his bed in the living room. It was natural for me to bond with everyone, and so I had no problems getting along with everyone.

In *Beat Instrumental* in June 1972, journalist John Bagnall, reported on the crowd who were waiting to get into the gig at Brighton's Dome Theatre:

Outside, the audience were already gathering. Judging from the snippets of conversation that I heard, there were many Curved Air followers. But there were many who seemed to be in my position. They'd heard all the praise for the band, but they remembered the period when Curved Air had been slated from all sides of the music business. Like me, they'd come to make their minds up. At one time not so long ago, it seemed the thing to knock Curved Air. They've evoked some bitter criticism in the past. Possibly more, in fact, than any other English rock band. I've always found it difficult to see the justification. Even if the packaging of Air Conditioning was gimmicky and the quality of the pressing poor, the music it contained, I've always felt, was vastly more inventive than that produced on so many other first albums. But the spectre of the first album proved difficult to lay to rest. The music press – which had been quick to hail the arrival of Curved Air – began to criticise the band as a hyped-up success. They were described as pretentious and over-musical. They earned no love through the fact that they apparently ignored the critics. There was also the success of 'Back Street Luv' – the cry of 'sellout!' might be a cliché, but anti-single prejudices still abound.

Bagnall's description of how he felt people perceived Curved Air by 1972 seems like a pretty fair assessment, suggesting that there were many things Curved Air had done in their tenure so far that invited criticism. As for advocating that 'Back Street Luv' ran the risk of the band being labelled as sellouts, well, maybe it's one of those cases of you're damned if you do and you're damned if you don't. Still though, by the time it came to making *Phantasmagoria* in 1972 – after getting the public's attention with their picture disc and having had success with the single of 'Back Street Luv' – Curved Air certainly still had everything to play for.

Phantasmagoria was recorded at Advision Studios in London, a mainstay recording facility for many progressive rock bands such as Yes, Gentle Giant and Emerson, Lake & Palmer. The album was produced by Colin Caldwell, who had also worked on *Air Conditioning* and *Second Album*. The cover illustration was by John Gorham, with beautiful lettering and a hooded creature smoking a hookah outdoors. *Phantasmagoria* was released in April 1972, entering the UK charts on 13 May and climbing up to number 20. The band went on a small tour of the US and UK and made a number of international television appearances.

With promotional activity as active as ever, Curved Air were featured on a flexi disc that came free with *New Musical Express*. The respective *NME* issue was advertised in the *Daily Mirror* in April 1972. The twelve-minute maxi-single had The Rolling Stones on the A-side, and Slade, Fanny and Curved Air on the B-side. The title track from *Phantasmagoria* represented Curved Air. Times were certainly busy in the run-up to the release of the *Phantasmagoria* album, as was reported in *The Birmingham Post* on Wednesday 29 March 1972:

> A substitute pop group, Argent, will appear instead of Curved Air at Birmingham Town Hall tonight. A spokesman for the Adlew Agency – Curved Air's managers – said they were stranded in West Germany because they had too much equipment to take on a passenger aircraft and had to wait for a freight flight today.

With the latter accounted for, when it came to making their third album, Curved Air were more established and experienced and in a better place professionally to put the full extent of confident creativity into their work. Sonja Kristina told *Beat Instrumental* in June 1972:

The first album was recorded the first time we'd ever been in a studio, and the second album was produced under a great deal of pressure. But this one was recorded under better circumstances. We knew when and how it was to be recorded and the whole thing was done in two weeks over the end of February.

It could be considered that *Phantasmagoria* was Curved Air's opportunity to really show what they were capable of without the pressures of publicity and criticism. In the same feature, Sonja Kristina continued:

It's *(Phantasmagoria)* representative of the differences in musical direction within the band. It's more relaxed. We've been through a lot of pressures. The new album is what's come out of it. The numbers are a matter of personal taste. We haven't made any compromises. We didn't set out with the deliberate intention of making *Phantasmagoria* the best album we could produce; we only set out to record what was there in the ideas of the band. But I think it is our best, and we are very pleased with that should it turn out that way.

Mike Wedgwood was Ian Eyre's replacement. Wedgwood contributed some great bass lines to *Phantasmagoria*. He had joined Curved Air not long before the recording of the album, and he certainly made his mark. Years later, he recalled his audition with the band as an unforgettable experience. Present at the audition was Sonja Kristina, Francis Monkman, Darryl Way and Florian Pilkington-Miksa. Monkman recalled playing loudly as he was asked to sight-read and play a complicated line of music in a complex time signature on the spot. Once he had gotten through it, he began to relax and they all started playing improvised pieces and a couple of Curved Air numbers. Sonja Kristina told *Disc* in April 1972:

Everything's fine now, just fine. The business is my whole life; really I couldn't exist any other way. I couldn't get any other sort of job. I love the ups and downs, it brings out the fighting side in you. We were very, very rushed 'round the period of the second album. We had to leave for our first tour of America the day after the album was mixed, and you're not really in a very stable state of mind when you're working all over the place so hard. But this time, we did nothing but rehearse, do the album and enjoy it, and because of the way we recorded it with a completely relaxed atmosphere, the album has that feel. With the first album, we were new to the studio. With the second one, we were in the middle of everything – tired, worried and everyone saying we had so much to prove, which reflected in the material. With this album, we knew what we wanted to do, and the feel of the album is far more relaxed, happier and more enjoyable. It's got a tremendous variety. I've done one of my own songs, which is nice for me, and they've added their musical bits and turned it into a complete Curved Air number, which would have never have been possible until I first met them … Now we've finished this album, we've got a whole lot of ideas for the next album. Recording is completely different from working on stage. You've written the material and then it develops and you develop too.

Curved Air's third album continued in the musical style of their previous albums insofar as it being comfortably classifiable as progressive rock. Some consider it to be their most sophisticated set of songs, showcasing the writing and performing talents of all members of the band. Journalist, John Bagnall, said of *Phantasmagoria* in *Beat Instrumental* in June 1972:

Certainly, *Phantasmagoria* is something of a departure from Curved Air's previous albums. The approach is more relaxed; the tempo is less frenetic. Listen to 'Melinda (More Or Less)', a simple song sung by Sonja with just the barest suggestion of Curved Air's normal instrumentation in the background. It works. The whole album works. It's toned-down considerably from the furious virtuosity of the previous albums, yet none of the excitement of Curved Air's musicianship has been lost. The whole album, I feel, is more successful for the fact that the music is more mellow and the band, somehow, more mature.

The paranormal themes of *Phantasmagoria* are stark and provocative. Sometimes it seems that Curved Air's songs are full of imagery of phantoms. Sonja Kristina told *The Arts Desk* in April 2014:

Francis' phantoms – they're his own – are all over *Phantasmagoria*. 'Over And Above' is a beautiful song; I can feel that when I sing it. Francis also wrote 'Everdance' on *Second Album* as well, but *Phantasmagoria* was the real ghost album.

Curved Air were at the peak of their success in 1972, appearing on many TV shows. The album's title track was performed on Austrian TV just before the band broke up in October of that year. The title, *Phantasmagoria*, came from Lewis Carroll's poem of the same name; his longest. The name means a sequence of frightening or fantastic images, as in a dream. The lyric sheet contains a quote from the poem:

Oh, when I was a little Ghost,
A merry time had we!
Each seated on his favourite post,
We chumped and chawed the buttered toast
They gave us for our tea.

Phantasmagoria is notable for its early use of the EMS Synthi 100 synthesizer, used to process Sonja Kristina's vocals when she recited the poem. The EMS was a large analogue/digital hybrid made by Electronic Music Studios (London) Ltd. The analogue and digital engineering was considered to be groundbreaking at the time. It was designed by David Cockerell in 1971 and was thus in its infancy when used by Curved Air. It was an expensive piece of kit, costing £6,500 at the time. The last unit built by EMS was number 30. Afterwards, one final unit was built by Datanomics, who bought assets from EMS when the company folded in 1979. Although the EMS Synthi 100 had a relatively short commercial lifespan, Curved Air's use of it was very much in line with their innovative approach to embracing technology in their music.

The band embraced a fair amount of technology when it came to doing their live shows too. In *Beat Instrumental* in June 1972, journalist, John Bagnall listed the equipment that was being prepared on stage prior to a gig at The Dome Theatre in Brighton's town centre: Ampeg bottoms with Hi-watt, Fender and Ampeg tops, a six-hundred-watt WEM PA augmented by Fender W-cabinets, three Audiomasters (one of which was exclusively used for micing up the drums), a WEM Reverbmaster and two WEM Copycat echo units (admittedly, most of that means little to me as narrator of this book, but I have included the information because I trust it could easily be of relevance and interest to some). Equally, the onstage instrumentation reflected Curved Air's preferred technology. For the gig reported on in *Beat Instrumental*, the stage was set up with an electric piano and VCS3 synthesizer, a small sound laboratory of various keyboards that included a Hammond organ, another VCS3, a specially made sequencer unit – oh, and more keyboards!

It is worth noting that Curved Air were not to everyone's taste when it came to their live performances. Understandably, of course, the technical demands of what the band did on record perhaps didn't always translate too well to the stage. In May 1972, *Record Mirror* reported on a performance that took place at Alexandra Palace:

It is sad, but there is something rather boring about the Curved Air live appearances. Certainly, on record, their music is imaginative and stimulating, but on stage – despite the banks of controls set in the auditorium – it seems impossible for the band to do justice to Sonja Kristina's voice. Sonja was frequently lost amid the whirling of notes from guitar, bass and organ/synthesizer. The words were never plain. The vocals from new member, Mike Wedgewood, on bass, were non-existent. Sad again, because he seems to have slipped so neatly into the group. So we sit and wait patiently for something to happen that will stir the large audience – shrunk by the vastness of Alexandra Palace – into some sort of enthusiasm. It finally comes of course with 'Vivaldi', the incredible synthesized fiddling of Darryl Way, and the synthesized synthesizing of Francis Monkman in a great baroque sound extravaganza.

Plans were actually in place to expand the stage show complexities. Way told *Record Mirror* in June 1972:

After that initial boom, there was a bit of a lull, but I think now we've got rid of the hype syndrome. We've been better on live dates during our last tour. We're happier with our music, and I think we've achieved a 100 per cent improvement on the old set. We've got a slick stage now. Some people would knock that, but I don't think there's anything wrong with being slick – it leaves so much more room to concentrate on the music. Our improvement on stage is partly a reflection of a more mature relationship among the group. For the future, I think we'll become a lot more exciting and visually spectacular. We've been thinking a lot about that lately. One way is to have our own light show travelling with us for all of our gigs – at the moment we hire lights for a tour – and make use of pre-recorded tapes.

The opening track on *Phantasmagoria* – 'Marie Antoinette' – tells the story of the rise and fall of the last queen of France before the French Revolution. Sonja Kristina told *Let It Rock* in August 2008:

> The sixties were revolutionary times. 'Marie Antoinette' was a symbol of social divisions that create unrest and the catalyst for change and evolution. With 'Propositions', I think Francis made a start on the song; then I played with the concept of annihilation. Wordplay out of which some kind of sense emerged.

'Marie Antoinette' added a touch of historical and gothic grandeur. It is certainly thunderous and attention-grabbing. Whilst, in contrast, the pastoral 'Melinda (More Or Less)' perhaps should have taken the group beyond being seen as one-hit-wonders, as they were by many.

'Melinda (More Or Less)' is the only song on the album composed entirely by Sonja Kristina. On *Phantasmagoria*, it could be considered that her folk roots really started to come to the fore. The song was first introduced to the band a couple of years earlier when they auditioned Sonja. She wrote the song in 1967 when she was eighteen and performing in small folk clubs. Sonja was always the main lyric writer in Curved Air, but 'Melinda (More Or Less)' was the first composition that was exclusively hers that the band recorded. The song gets an excellent treatment, the band really doing the emotion in the lyrics, justice. Francis Monkman plays sentimental harpsichord lines in the background, whilst Darryl Way shines with his violin accompaniment and solo. A distinctive feature of the song is the interplay between the violin and flute played by Annie Stewart. Sonja Kristina's acoustic guitar and voice on the track is such that it is easy to picture her performing the song solo in a folk club in 1967.

'Not Quite The Same' begins with medieval brass sounds before flourishing into a bouncy folk-jazz with a melancholy chorus. Unusually, both Way and Monkman play synthesizer on this track. 'Cheetah' is an upbeat Darryl Way instrumental that has him starring on violin. There are plenty of unpredictable changes in the piece to keep it interesting. Francis Monkman dazzles on 'Ultra Vivaldi', where he gives an electronic take on 'Vivaldi' on the VCS3 synthesizer.

The vinyl's second side starts with the album's title song. It's in a playful style, with fantasy-based lyrics and an intelligent use of structure and melody that add to the mood of the piece. The next track – 'Whose

Shoulder Are You Looking Over Anyway?' – is a three-minute-long atmospheric piece that perhaps doesn't stand as a solitary tune but does seem to function as an introduction to the song that follows it. 'Over And Above' is an eight-minute-long epic: a magnificent concoction created by Francis Monkman. Jazz percussionist, Frank Ricotti, can be heard prominently on this track playing xylophone and vibraphone: instruments you do not usually hear in popular music. Around the time of recording the album, Ricotti was in the band of jazz orchestrator Michael Gibbs. The jazz influences in the song are certainly noticeable – an intriguing combination of jazz and symphonic rock with effective parts written for the brass instruments. The wild and unpredictable feel of the album is exemplified in the concluding track, 'Once A Ghost, Always A Ghost': an unusual brassy cabaret-style song. It ends the album on an offbeat yet thought-provoking note, thanks in part to another incredible vibraphone solo.

Phantasmagoria was reviewed in *Beat Instrumental* in June 1972:

If *Air Conditioning* was an outstanding first album, then Curved Air's *Phantasmagoria* must put many third albums in the shade. It displays a musical maturity beyond the band's two years of existence. It is possibly more relaxed than the first two albums and has gained immeasurably for that one simple fact. The one fault of the previous offerings was that the sheer virtuosity of the performance sometimes disguised the guts implicit in Curved Air's music. *Phantasmagoria* reasserts the balance. An excellent album, powerfully written, played and produced to Curved Air's impeccable standards.

It was reviewed in *Disc* in April 1972:

Wham! The band's third album is quite a slayer. It doesn't bash you over the head with uncontrolled power, but it creeps into the psyche menacingly – out to haunt like a Hitchcock shadow. They're masters of the ethereal sound and here it is developed to perfection, especially on side two with synthesizer supremo, Francis Monkman, lurking eerily throughout, combining with Darryl Way's seething violin to provide the backdrop for Sonja Kristina's clear vocals to deliver the surreal, almost paranoid lyrics conjuring images of an Alice lost in the Chamber of Horrors. The second side is all Monkman, with the synthesizer dominating. There are some strange noises created, very murky –

especially on 'Whose Shoulder Are You Looking Over Anyway?' and likewise 'Once A Ghost, Always A Ghost'. Side one – featuring the Way/ Linwood compositions – is another story, far more lyrical and melodic in content, less Moog, yet retaining the band's characteristic depth. The six-odd minutes of 'Marie Antoinette' builds dramatically then drops down into the album's most lilting piece, 'Melinda (More Or Less)'. Watch out on this side, too, for the way Darryl's violin literally darts from speaker to speaker at the climax of 'Ultra Vivaldi'.

The album's title track, 'Phantasmagoria', was used as the B-side of the single release, 'Sarah's Concern'. The *Coventry Evening Telegraph* reviewed 'Sarah's Concern' in April 1972:

Folk music by any other name, even with its freaky electronics and artificial harmonies. Surprising, really, that the group should have had so much success – they must have the folk purists muttering through their beards and most pop fans totally bemused. Yet their last album earned them a silver disc for 250,000 sales. Their six-week tour of Britain should enhance the chances of their new single, and a hit for that would also be a surprise.

By 1972, Curved Air had a solid reputation as a live band. In August 1972, the *Reading Evening Post* featured a review of their performance at the Reading festival:

It's really quite something when the attention of 5,000 or so rock fans in the freezing dead of night can be held by one man with a violin, especially when that man happens to be playing the winter overture from Vivaldi's *Four Seasons*. Yet that's how Darryl Way, violinist with Curved Air, stole the show on the opening night of the Thames-side rock festival. It was quite an experience. Starting as a fairly straight copy of the original classic, it moved into some pretty skull-crunching electronics. There was some ear-piercing feedback building up to breaking point, about ninety seconds of electronic screeching until Darryl Way, calm and controlled, held the electric violin aloft and blew it to pieces in his hand. Then, amazingly, he picked up another instrument and the band came in behind him to finish the piece in grand style. Cries for more echoed into the night. Curved Air were great from the moment they came on. Running through some numbers from their first album and the hit single, 'Back Street Luv', they were always in control. Sonja Kristina, the band's singer, said she was suffering from tonsillitis. No one could have noticed as she raised her voice and the crowd's spirits into the night. She sings well, has a deft touch on the guitar and looks absolutely delicious. Together with the band, she effectively wiped out the memories of the earlier groups. A pity, perhaps, because Mungo Jerry, who went before, weren't all that bad.

Curved Air's performance at The Dome Theatre in Brighton was reviewed in *Beat Instrumental* in June 1972:

On stage, Gary Moore – late of Skid Row – had finished his loud and powerful set, leaving Darryl Way struggling to do up the zip on an impossibly tight pair of white trousers. At the mixing desk, I waited to see just how good or bad, Curved Air were. The lights eventually dimmed to leave the hall and the stage in darkness. The two-thousand-seater Dome was about two-thirds full. A stereo tape desk was switched on and the hall filled with the sounds of a pre-recorded synthesizer tape. A buzz of excitement ran through the audience. Suddenly the stage lights came blazing on and Darryl Way, Francis Monkman, Mike Wedgwood and Florian Pilkington-Miksa swung into the opening bars of 'Cheetah'. The number finished with the stage again in darkness. Two white spotlights played on the background curtains as Sonja entered. Showmanship certainly, but the audience loved it. 'And now', said Sonja, 'Welcome to our Phantasmagoria!' and sang to the bass accompaniment of Mike Wedgwood. The reception was phenomenal. Curved Air followed with 'Marie Antoinette' and the single, 'Sarah's Concern'; introduced to a barrage of ironic cheering by Sonja, as 'uncontaminated by Radio One's little fingers': a reference, in fact, to the BBC's refusal – for reasons best known to itself – not to play the single unless it makes the top 30. 'Piece Of Mind' from the second album followed, and still I wasn't quite sure whether I liked the band or not. But 'Vivaldi' clinched it. Darryl Way's arrangement – and Curved Air's piece de resistance – must now rank on the same level as The Nice' 'America' and Hendrix's 'Purple Haze' when it comes to showstoppers. Way, staggering over the stage like the devil himself, played the number to perfection. The excitement built up through Monkman's synthesizer solo and the ear-shattering climax. As Curved Air left the stage, the audience were up on their feet, pressing forward to the stage in defiance of those gloomy (venue regulation) warnings. Curved Air came back to play 'Everdance'. The audience were dancing all over the hall, following Sonja as she led them. As the number returned to the 'Vivaldi' theme, Monkman passed the synthesizer keyboard to the audience, a novel variation on the concept of participation. A second encore was a certainty; 'What do you do in the morning?' shouted Sonja. 'Stretch!' screamed the audience. And 'Stretch' ended the set. The audience stood clapping and cheering for a further ten minutes before drifting happily away. Apparently, it's a familiar scene. Whatever Curved Air were in the past – hype or supergroup – they've now emerged as one of the most mature, exciting and musical bands on the UK rock circuits. I left Brighton well and truly converted.

As with 1970 and 1971, Curved Air were often on the same bill as many other high profile groups. *Record Mirror* reported in August 1972:

The final line-up for the eleventh National Jazz & Blues Festival was announced last week. To be held next weekend at the same Reading site used for last year's event, the three-day festival features some of the best British acts on the road at the moment. Friday's bill, which starts at 4 p.m., stars Curved Air, with Mungo Jerry, Genesis, Jackson Heights, Nazareth and Steamhammer. The following day, The Faces top the bill in a programme that starts at noon, which also features the Electric Light Orchestra, Focus, The Edgar Broughton Band, If, Linda Lewis, Man and, from America, The Johnny Otis Show. Jonathan Kelly completes the line-up. Sunday's programme, which also starts at noon, stars Ten Years After, Status Quo, Quintessence, Roy Wood's Wizard, Stray, Matching Mole, Vinegar Joe, Gillian McPherson and Stackridge.

An adventurous album, *Phantasmagoria* was the group's last to dent the top 20. Once again, the record's track order was split between Way and Monkman on side one and two of the LP, respectively. In some ways, *Phantasmagoria* signified the end of an era for Curved Air. There were musical differences present that ultimately led to the break-up of the band as it was known at the time. Some suggested that Darryl Way was something of a perfectionist. Upon being asked about what she made of Way's perfectionism, Sonja Kristina told *Hit Channel* in December 2018:

I think he wanted us to be perfectionists, for him, because he couldn't bear to hear live recordings because he thought they were imperfect and they couldn't be improved. When we performed the songs, the shows all went down really, really well and he played beautifully. He became more perfectionist after he left and built a studio at home, where he could just redo things over and over until they are perfect.

By October of 1972, the original Curved Air line-up decided to call it quits. After three years of existence and constant touring, supporting and performing alongside acts such as Black Sabbath, Jethro Tull and Deep Purple, the founding members were exhausted by the rock 'n' roll experience. They were told at the time that if they just toured the US another three times before the spring, they had a reasonable chance of breaking just about even financially. But no, they had had enough by then. When Clifford Davis – Curved Air's manager after Mark Hanau – clarified for them what they would have to do in terms of touring, just to get somewhere near financially even, the enormity of the whole thing certainly seemed to contribute towards a feeling of burnout. Sonja Kristina alluded to the scale of the band's contractual obligations in *Disc & Music Echo* in January 1971:

> I'll be with Curved Air for three years at least, because we have a contract which ties us for that time. It's a good idea being contracted because we know we have to be together, and so there has to be a lot more give and take and we can't afford to fall out with each other – we don't want to anyway. But there's so much talent in the group that if we did split, there would be at least four different bands.

She wasn't wrong.

By the end of 1972, Francis Monkman self-admitted to being a nervous wreck, on the verge of physical and mental breakdown. He had to wear earplugs to go on the London Underground and went to a naturopath three times a week. Years later, in one interview, Mike Wedgwood recalled that Curved Air was a very intense band in terms of the music, but also in terms of personality, and this was particularly exacerbated by life on the road. In a world of fast cars, stage-door exit madness and wild clothes, it had reached the point of all being a bit too much. Still, Sonja Kristina remained invested in the band. She told *Disc* in April 1972:

> I'd love another child, but at this present juncture, I couldn't see it happening. Even if the whole Curved Air thing fell through, I'd get an incredible urge to get up fighting again.

A talent unto themselves, both Darryl Way and Francis Monkman contributed so much creativity and musical innovation to *Phantasmagoria*, but sadly perhaps, as individuals, they were tired of the musical direction that the band was going in overall; they were at odds with each other and the band. The result of this was for them both to leave for solo and session ventures. By the end of the tour to promote *Phantasmagoria*, Monkman and Way wanted out. Essentially, they were moving in completely different musical directions. Florian Pilkington-Miksa also left the band. After apparently giving minimal notice, he eventually joined Kiki Dee's band.

In all fairness, Darryl Way said from the start that he wasn't enthusiastic about Curved Air's touring commitments in terms of having to go to America. He expressed his thoughts on the tour that Curved Air were about to do (a two month coast-to-coast trip of America) to *Beat Instrumental* in March 1971:

> Personally, I don't want to go. I just don't fancy the idea of America; it seems too big and impersonal. I'm very English – attached to the English soil. I'm also apprehensive at the thought of flying, but there's no room for phobias in the band; it's got to be done.

Still, it wasn't to be the end of the road for Curved Air as a recognised band. *The Liverpool Echo* reported in October 1972:

> A big shock for Liverpool Curved Air fans is this week's news that Darryl Way and Francis Monkman are to leave. They will be replaced by seventeen-year-old Eddie Jobson from Newcastle, who plays violin, keyboards and synthesizer, and 'Kirby', who is a well-known session musician.

The media interest in Sonja Kristina as an individual artist perhaps aided her in being able to keep Curved Air going into the following year. *Melody Maker* placed an advert in the *Daily Mirror* in June 1972. The advert described Sonja Kristina:

> A chick on the road – Sonja Kristina has been called 'the female Mick Jagger'; her wild stage act is one of the reasons why her band, Curved Air, is one of Britain's foremost rock attractions. Last weekend, *Melody Maker* travelled with them on a typical gig. This week, we tell you about it. *Melody Maker*, get it today, 7p.

In *Disc* in April 1972, Sonja Kristina described what it was like being in the industry as a woman:

Ninety per cent of the time, I don't worry about it, but then if you get a bit reflective or despondent, you worry about being a woman, about people saying you ought to be more ladylike. You see a very attractive woman with a lot of make-up on and think, 'Should I be like that?', but I can't be bothered. I think with make-up and things, if women do it, why shouldn't a man do it too – it's nice to make up. Or everyone just paint their faces for fun. The trouble with make-up is you can't touch your eyes because you'll smudge it, and it all runs when you get hot, so I end up looking like a panda. All these things are problems – the way you're supposed to dress to be a star. What you wear really doesn't matter – if people despise you for what you're wearing, then they can't be very nice people in the first place.

It seems that Curved Air were quite the stylish band when it came to fashion. In *Beat Instrumental* in June 1972, journalist John Bagnall, noted how everyone was dressed when they arrived at the venue to prepare for the gig:

The battery of stage lights which Curved Air now incorporate into their stage act had just been hauled into position when the band arrived. Darryl Way was wearing a light brown suit, Sonja Kristina was resplendent in her multi-coloured jacket and midi. Francis Monkman looked like a cavalier with his wide-brimmed hat and knee-length boots.

It also comes across that Curved Air were quite an eccentric band to meet. At least, that seems to be how Bagnall described them in the same feature:

Curved Air prepared to run through a few numbers. When Sonja tuned the guitar that she has lately begun to feature on stage, Darryl was seeking out someone who knew the town: 'Is there a sports shop anywhere 'round here?', he asked – 'I want to buy an air rifle'. The reason, Sonja explained, was that there had been an intruder at their flat the night before, and Darryl was the only member who would be returning to London after the evening's concert. 'He's feeling a bit nervous', she smiled. The soundcheck over, the band returned to their hotel, while Darryl – with personal manager Mal – went in search of his air rifle. The roadies made the final checks, adjusted the position of the PA to get the best vocal distribution, and switched on the synthesizers to warm the circuits: a move, I was told, that prevented them from going out of tune too quickly during the performance.

1973

Air Cut

Personnel:

Sonja Kristina: lead (1-4, 6, 8) and backing (7) vocals, acoustic guitar (2)

Eddie Jobson: electric violin, backing vocals (6), VCS3 synthesizer, Mellotron, pianos, organ, harpsichord (2)

Kirby Gregory: electric and bass (4) guitars, backing vocals

Mike Wedgwood: bass (all but 4) and acoustic (4) guitars, backing and lead vocals (7, 8)

Jim Russell: drums

Artwork design: Modula

Artwork illustration based on drawing by Ian Fink

Engineer: Paul 'The Rock' Hardiman

Photography: Mal Linwood-Ross and Mike Putland

Studio: Advision Studios, London

Producer: Martin Rushent

Highest chart places: UK: Did not chart

Side One. 1. 'The Purple Speed Queen' (Kristina, Kirby) 3:20, 2. 'Elfin Boy' (Kristina, Jobson) 4:20, 3. 'Metamorphosis' (Kristina, Jobson) 10:30, 4. 'World' (Wedgwood) 1:32

Side Two 5. 'Armin' (Jobson, Wedgwood, Kirby, Russell) 3:16, 6. 'U.H.F.' (Kirby) 6:06, 7. 'Two-Three-Two' (Wedgwood) 4:10, 8. 'Easy' (Kristina) 6:45

Through the early-1970s, Curved Air had achieved success with the release of their first three studio albums, *Air Conditioning*, *Second Album*, and *Phantasmagoria*. They had toured with artists such as Black Sabbath, B.B. King, Deep Purple, Jethro Tull, The Who and Procol Harum, to name a few. Curved Air had toured widely in the UK and twice in the States. All in all, they had certainly made their mark both musically and commercially. But the beginning of 1973 presented Sonja Kristina with dilemma and worry, in the form of how she could maintain Curved Air with the founding members having left the band at the end of 1972. She told *Melody Maker* in May 1973:

> I was having nightmares just before the old band broke up. I was beginning to feel incredibly insecure about the whole future. I realised that with Darryl and Francis gone, Curved Air's future was my responsibility.

Despite *Phantasmagoria* having been met with critical acclaim, the musical differences between Francis Monkman and Darryl Way were such that the album's line-up was no longer sustainable. The divisions had been there since *Second Album*, as was implied in how the individual writer's tracks were split between sides one and two of both *Second Album* and *Phantasmagoria*. Although *Phantasmagoria* had reached number 20 in the UK charts by the end of 1972, Darryl Way had formed his own band, Wolf, and Francis Monkman went to work with Al Stewart on his fifth studio album, *Past, Present And Future*, and Lynsey de Paul's debut album, *Surprise*, in 1973. Way told *Goldmine* in September 2018:

> Francis went his way and I went mine. With Wolf, I wanted to create an instrumental band.

In *Melody Maker* in May 1973, Sonja Kristina philosophised on the break-up post *Phantasmagoria*:

> There were silly arguments between us over the business side of the band. The friction between us was quite pointless, because as musicians, we didn't have control over it. I think it was because we all had new bands on our minds. Darryl didn't want to let the band down, so he stayed behind to gig with us until we found a replacement. At the same time, he was rehearsing Wolf, so he didn't get any free time. At that time, I was taking a big step musically. I was frightened of being left in command, yet it was what I wanted and needed because Darryl and Francis had always had strict control over the band's musical policy. I think that if they hadn't got out, then I would have quit the band. I was becoming more and more restricted in what I was allowed to do.

From Curved Air's point of view, after *Phantasmagoria*, the only remaining members in the band were Sonja Kristina and Mike Wedgwood. They both decided on a new line-up which featured Kirby Gregory on guitar, Jim Russell on drums, and the debut of a pre-Roxy-Music Eddie Jobson on keyboards and violin. The fourth studio album, *Air Cut*, was originally released in early 1973 on the Warner Bros. label. Jim Russell and Kirby Gregory had already been active with Curved Air in late 1972 during the last leg of the UK *Phantasmagoria* tour. They stayed on after the tour to become full band members in 1973. Kirby told *Guitar* in July 1973:

Jim Russell, the drummer, and I joined last October and we did a tour with Darryl Way. Then Darryl left the band and Eddie Jobson came in. He plays electric violin, piano, organ, synthesizer and Mellotron. We did a tour of Italy, just to warm up, then we made the album (*Air Cut*), and then did a tour of England.

Sonja Kristina said of Kirby in *Melody Maker* in May 1973:

He takes his music very seriously, just as Darryl and Francis both did, but what he likes, they wouldn't consider valid.

In *Record Collector* in April 2012, Sonja explained how the musical differences between Darryl Way and Francis Monkman came more to light during the making of *Phantasmagoria*, and how this inspired the new line-up for 1973:

Those two were in charge of most of the music, but were heading in different directions. A split, though inevitable, was amicable. Kirby Gregory, who replaced Francis, was quite spectacular – wild, fast, furious – while Eddie Jobson had supported Curved Air in Newcastle a couple of times with a local band, Fat Grapple. As he'd been influenced by Darryl, he knew the pieces, including 'Vivaldi', and with Darryl's blessing, we invited him to join. It was all very seamless. We were able to carry on working, and we wrote and recorded *Air Cut*.

All things considered, it seems justified that a new Curved Air line-up was in place by the point at which *Air Cut* was to be made. As was reported in *Beat Instrumental* in December 1972:

Kirby Gregory had a phone call one day from Sonja Kristina. She'd been given his name from a mutual friend and wanted to know whether he was interested in auditioning for Curved Air. After three minutes of playing, he'd found himself a job as lead guitarist with Curved Air. Until that time, he hadn't given much thought to the music of Curved Air. He'd heard their albums but had never actually bought one. A month before he actually played with the band, he was taken to a gig which he thoroughly enjoyed. After a few such visits, he was confident enough to step up and join the encore. The vacancy which Gregory filled came up when Francis Monkman decided to leave the band due to musical differences.

At around the same time, Darryl Way expressed the possibility that he too would leave in the near future, and seventeen-year-old wonder, Eddie Jobson, was recruited in preparation. Monkman didn't leave as soon as he'd made the decision but stayed on until Gregory felt confident enough to make his live debut. Gregory is nineteen years old.

Kirby asserted in the same feature: 'I really like the first album and I'd seen them on TV a few times. I'd always thought they were pretty good, but I'd never seen them live'.

In *Guitar* in July 1973, Kirby described the band's writing process:

We all write separately and we've tried all the combinations of writing together. Like, on the last album, we wrote a song each, and I wrote one with Sonja – 'Purple Speed Queen'. And there was one group composition, 'Armin'. When we went to Italy, we had to chuck a set together quickly, and we wrote that number at our first rehearsal. When I write a song, I think of it right from the beginning as it will eventually sound. I don't write for the band like, I don't think, 'we've got a violin in the band, so I'll write something for the violin', and because Eddie plays a wide range of instruments, that's alright. If he just played the violin, a lot of stuff I write we just couldn't do. Because we have such a diverse attitude to music, it takes a little more time than it would if we all liked the same things. But it has its advantages too. Basically, whoever writes the song, brings in his tape recording of it, then we work on it together. For the album, we knew most of the numbers well when we went into the studio, but not too well – we hadn't flogged them to death. And there were a couple of things we actually wrote in the studio. A lot of things on *Air Cut* were spontaneous, if not truly improvised. When we rehearsed for the record, we all played as much as we could on each number, tried every possible thing we could do with them. Then when we got into the studio, we sort of filtered things out and channelled them into different directions.

Kirby told *Beat Instrumental* in December 1972:

In the early days, I used to learn the chords to songs. It was a very slow process. It suddenly dawned on me that there was more to guitar-playing than stringing chords together. I went through lots of stages as I developed. I practice a lot, at least an hour a day. Now I just concentrate

Above: The 1971 line up. From left to right: Francis Monkman, Florian Pilkington-Miksa, Ian Eyre, Sonja Kristina and Darryl Way.

Below: The 1976 line up. From left to right: Mick Jacques, Sonja Kristina, Tony Reeves, Stewart Copeland and Darryl Way.

Left: The cover for the band's debut album *Air Conditioning*, released in 1970. (*Warner Brothers*)

Right: *Second Album* was released in 1971 and included the band's only UK hit, 'Back Street Luv'. (*Warner Brothers*)

Right: The band's third album was *Phantasmagoria*, released in 1972. (*Warner Brothers*)

Left: *Air Cut* was the band's fourth album, released in 1973. Produced by Martin Rushent, it was the band's first album not to chart in the UK. (*Warner Brothers*)

Left: Sonja Kristina performing 'Back Street Luv' on the German TV show *Beat Club* in 1971.

Right: Some nifty video effects show Sonja and Francis Monkman during the same performance on *Beat Club* in 1971.

Left: Darryl Way, Ian Eyre and Florian Pilkington-Miksa performing 'It Happened Today' on the German TV show *Beat Club* in 1971.

Right: Sonja performing 'It Happened Today' in 1971.

Left: Darryl and Ian on the German TV show *Beat Club* in 1971.

Right: Florian during the same performance of 'It Happened Today' on the German TV show *Beat Club* in 1971.

Left: Sonja performing 'Prepositions' also on the German TV show *Beat Club* in 1971.

Right: Francis launches into a synth solo during the same performance of 'Prepositions' in 1971.

Left: The entire five-piece performing on the German TV show *Beat Club* in 1971.

Right: Sonja mimes to 'Phantasmagoria' on *Beat Club* in 1972.

Left: A very glamorous-looking Sonja performing 'Melinda' on the Austrian TV show, *Spotlight* in October 1972.

Right: Darryl Way playing with passion during the same performance of 'Melinda' in 1972.

Left: *Midnight Wire* was released in 1975. It was the first album by the 'new look' Curved Air, with only Sonja Kristina and Darryl Way present from the line up from the previous year. (*BTM*)

Right: The band's final album of the 1970s was *Airborne*, released in 1976. It marked Stewart Copeland's debut as a songwriter. (*BTM*)

Right: *Curved Air Live* was recorded at the end of 1974 and released in 1975. (*BTM*)

Left: *Live At The BBC* was a compilation of sessions and live performances between 1970 and 1976, released in 1995. (*Band Of Joy*)

11TH NATIONAL JAZZ·BLUES·FOLK & ROCK FESTIVAL

Again at the beautiful **THAMES-SIDE** arena and camp site

READING

An NJF/MARQUEE presentation · BERKSHIRE

11 AUGUST
Friday
from
4 p.m.

CURVED AIR - MUNGO JERRY
GENESIS . PRETTY THINGS . NAZARETH
STEAM HAMMER . Cottonwood. Etc.

12 AUGUST
Saturday
from
Noon

THE FACES
ELECTRIC LIGHT ORCHESTRA . FOCUS
EDGAR BROUGHTON . IF . LINDA LEWIS
Man . Mahatma Kane Jeeves . Jericho.
Jonathan Kelly . Solid Gold Cadillac. Etc.
and special Guests from the U.S.A.
THE JOHNNY OTIS R & B SHOW
with **Shuggie Otis and the Three Tons of Joy**

13 AUGUST
Sunday
from
Noon

TEN YEARS AFTER
QUINTESSENCE . Roy Wood's WIZARD
STATUS QUO . MATCHING MOLE . STRAY
Vinegar Joe . Gillian McPherson .
Sutherland Brothers . Stackridge .
Brewer's Droop . String Driven Thing . Etc.

TRAVEL Less than 40 miles
West of London New
Motorway M4 Section now
open. 30 minutes by train
from Paddington late trains.
Main station 10 min. walk.

★SPECIAL WEEKEND TICKETS
including Camping
and car parking at
no extra charge —
£3.25
★ *(IN ADVANCE ONLY)* ★

ADMISSION
AT GROUND
Friday: £1
Saturday: £1
Sunday: £1

Left: A promo poster for the eleventh Reading Festival from 1972, with Curved Air headlining the Friday night alongside Mungo Jerry. A remarkable evening's entertainment also included Genesis and Nazareth!

Right: An advert for a student gig from 1972 at the London College Of Printing.

LONDON COLLEGE OF PRINTING
Elephant and Castle Tube

Thursday, 24th February
JIMI HENDRIX FILM
CAT MOTHER + JIMMY & VELLA

Friday, 3rd March
in association with L.S.E.
THE JEFF BECK GROUP
+ HEAVEN

Saturday, 11th March
CURVED AIR
Lights — Bar — Disco
Tel. L.C.P.S.U. 01-735 6871 for further details

WORDS ST ALBANS CITY HALL
BARRY CLARKE

FRIDAY, 26th SEPTEMBER, 8.30 p.m. - 2 a.m.
LATE LATE ROCK SHOW II

CURVED AIR
ROGER RUSKIN SPEAR'S GIANT KINETIC WARDROBE
+ SQUEEZE + ACTRESS
Mary Jane Disco Bar till 1.30 a.m. Tickets from Box Office, Chequer St . St Albans
St Albans 64511

Left: An advert from a live appearance in 1975, with Squeeze on the undercard!

Above: A promo poster for Buxton Pop Festival in 1972. Another amazing line up also included performances from Slade, Steppenwolf, Uriah Heep, Family and Wishbone Ash.

Right: A promo poster from 1972 for some summer gigs in Hamilton, New Jersey, which saw Curved Air support Deep Purple in an astonishing line up of performances.

Right: Another concert advert, this time at The Roundhouse in London in 1976, saw the band share a stage with jazz-rockers Brand X.

Left: 'Back Street Luv' was released as a single in 1971 with 'Everdance' on the B-side. It reached number four in the UK charts. (*Warner Brothers*)

Right: 'Vivaldi' was released as a single in 1971 with 'It Happened Today' on the B-side. It didn't chart but was covered by Francis Monkman's band Sky on their album *Sky 2*, released in 1980. (*Warner Brothers*)

Left: 'Sarah's Concern' was released as a single in 1972 with 'Phantasmagoria' on the B-side. (*Warner Brothers*)

Right: Darryl Way's band Wolf released *Canis Lupus* in 1973. (*Esoteric*)

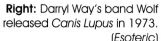

Left: Wolf's *Saturation Point* was released in 1973. (*Esoteric*)

Right: Darryl Way's classical *Concerto For Electric Violin* was released in 1978 and featured a synthesized orchestra played by Francis Monkman. (*Esoteric*)

Above: Sonja Kristina fronts the revived band, playing The Summers End Festival in Chepstow in October 2014. (*Photo credit: Richard Forster*)

Below: Kirby Gregory and Chris Harris playing The Summers End Festival in October 2014. (*Photo credit: Richard Forster*)

Above: Sonja watches violinist Paul Sax at The Summers End Festival in October 2014. (*Photo credit: Richard Forster*)

Below: The whole band take a bow after their performance at The Summers End Festival in October 2014. Also pictured are keyboard player Robert Norton and, of course, Florian Pilkington-Miksa. (*Photo credit: Richard Forster*).

Left: Such was the success of 'Back Street Luv' that session musicians covered it for release on one of Hallmark's *Top Of The Pops* LPs in 1971. (*Hallmark*)

Below: A ticket stub from a show at Bournemouth Winter Gardens in 1971.

WINTER GARDENS BOURNEMOUTH

Curved Air

at 7.45 p.m.
STALLS
90p

| | 24

The Promenade Bar (adjoining Theatre) Open from 6.0 p.m.
Tickets cannot be exchanged or Money refunded
To be retained

SAT
23rd
OCT
1971

THE DOME, BRIGHTON

THURSDAY, 5 APRIL, 1973
at 7.30 p.m.
(Doors open 7.00)

CURVED AIR

plus
SUPPORTING
ATTRACTION

ROW

F 39

BALCONY **60p**

This ticket subject to V.A.T. if purchased after 1st April

Tickets cannot be accepted for exchange or refund. Latecomers will not have access to their seats until a suitable interval.

TO BE RETAINED

Above: A ticket stub from a show at The Dome in Brighton during 1973.

Chess Janus Records
and
British Talent Managers
are proud to announce the birth
of a new label

BTM records

A dynamic new music force.

BTM Records launches its debut release with an important LP by Curved Air who have just concluded a highly successful UK tour. Curved Air's new LP is destined to add to their legend.

This is only the beginning... forthcoming releases include such acts as Caravan, Lucifer's Friend and American Gypsy.

Talent.
All part of a dynamic new music force.

BTM records

Right: BTM proudly announces Curved Air's 1975 live album. It didn't chart but did well enough to pay off the band's tax bill. (*BTM*)

on technicalities – scales. If you don't practice, you find yourself getting lazy. I still learn things off records; they're not usually guitar parts. It's more of a challenge to play sax parts, for instance, they're all in B flat! If you become really competent with your instrument, you get much more satisfaction from playing simple things.

At the time of the above interview, Kirby's guitar of choice was a Dan Armstrong plexiglass.

In their new form, Curved Air turned up the volume for *Air Cut*. Sonja Kristina told *Record Mirror* in January 1973:

The whole music scene is so pliable, it's difficult to get any clear picture. I think it'll be an important year for us, and I think Uriah Heep and Genesis are the bands to watch this year.

The album offers lots of creativity and certainly deserves to be heard. Eddie Jobson was recruited to replace Darryl Way on violin and keyboard duties. Jobson had big shoes to fill, but he was very much the capable candidate. That said, it is plausible that the pressure may have been on. Jobson told *Keyboard* in November 2016:

In the early days, being so diverse was probably detrimental to establishing my own musical identity, at least in the public's mind. In Curved Air, I had to replace two of my musical heroes, the main guys in my favourite group, so I was first seen as the seventeen-year-old 'Darryl Way/Francis Monkman replacement' kid.

Having joined the band at such a young age, Eddie Jobson was an impressive choice of new recruit. Sonja Kristina spoke highly of his contribution to *Air Cut*. She explained to *Goldmine* in March 2018:

Eddie Jobson was only seventeen when he joined Curved Air, when Darryl Way left for a while. He was a very talented boy, playing piano, violin and synthesizer. He came from Newcastle and heard ELP and Curved Air at the same time. He would buy those records, lift the needle off the vinyl, play his instrument and go back to the albums until he learned all the songs. Ultimately, we lost him to Roxy Music. He was spending a lot of time in the studio with Bryan Ferry. I wrote the lyrics to 'Metamorphosis', and all that music was young Eddie.

In *Melody Maker* in May 1973, Sonja explained how the new line-up managed to establish a rapport:

> We had to get to know each other as musicians. We worked hard to get a set together for our Italian tour, the whole time learning about our different ways. The tour turned out to be an incredible success. We came back and just split from each other for a week, the idea being that we could all work on material for the album. Both Kirby and Eddie came up with some good material. We were all working hard towards the album, and by the time we got into the studios, the whole band was becoming excited about the way things were going.

It comes across that the band's 1973 line-up had a good professional rapport. When asked by journalist, Pat Worship, how the band might manage any competition for solo spots, both in the recording studio and on stage at any given moment, Kirby told *Guitar* in July 1973:

> I think that's down to experience and self-control. In any case, there are only a couple of numbers in our set with open spaces where we can really let go and improvise. We all get our individual spotlight in the show, but in most of the numbers, there's a fairly tight framework to work in. Then again, that must be done sensibly. I've been in bands where everything has been so tightly-arranged that you forget the whole point of why you're there. I used to think that about Yes – that they were over-arranged and clinical. But after seeing them, I don't know. Either they are clinical, or they're just so good at what they're doing. That's the thing about technique too. You can use it in two ways: you can use it to prove yourself, or the way you should use it as a medium of expression. You can play a simple twelve-bar with a lot of feeling, but it's much harder to play something in 11/8 with a lot of feeling. That's where the technique comes in.

When asked in the same interview if there were any special problems that cropped up in terms of electric guitar and electric violin being played at the same time, Kirby said:

> I know what you mean; so many guitarists try to sound like violins anyway! No, no problems really, because we don't really play a lot together as far as soloing is concerned. We're very aware that we could

end up sounding like Wishbone Ash, with violin and guitar instead of two guitars. If we did do more, I'd like to do it Frank Zappa's way – he's done some great things with violin.

In the same feature, Kirby was also asked what his thoughts were on playing with synthesized sounds. He responded:

That's affected me a lot. There are really only three or four schools of synthesizer-playing. Eddie has his own style – he's not into the electronic side as much as getting nice melodies out of it. That's alright, I've adjusted to it, but I'm very wary of the traditional synthesizer sound. To me, it's completely boring. I tried playing guitar through a synthesizer. It took away all the subtleties you strive for when you play guitar – tone, vibrato and so on. It just makes it a keyboard with strings on. All the effects I use, it's been a slow learning process. Like, I first played wah-wah five years ago, but I didn't bother to use one up until about six months ago. Then I started to think about it more, and now I use it, but only for short little things.

Kirby Gregory and Jim Russell had joined Curved Air as a result of good auditions. The band had gelled on the road before entering the studio with producer Martin Rushent (in the liner notes, Curved Air credit him for making the recording of *Air Cut* a great experience). The songs are generally more concise than on Curved Air's earlier output, and the sound is more in line with that of heavy rock – you can feel the band shedding their progressive rock personae for a more mainstream rock one. 'Purple Speed Queen' is a powerful opener, rocking along nicely with particularly inspired solos from Eddie Jobson and Kirby Gregory. It kicks off the album with a sense of adventure. It is certainly attention-grabbing.

The delicate 'Elfin Boy' sees the band display a more intimate side, a great folk song enhanced by a nice arrangement. 'Metamorphosis' is arguably a highlight of the album in how it is unlike the other tracks. It maintains the progressive rock tradition of being an epic multi-part song with classical influences. The band's inventive arrangements – particularly Eddie Jobson's outstanding keyboard work – make it one of Curved Air's strongest tracks, both technically and creatively. Jobson shines on 'Metamorphosis', particularly in the opening piano solo. Mike Wedgwood's bass comes through sturdily, prior to Jobson playing throughout various sections between the organ and VCS3, as if he's floating high up into the heavens, moving smoothly from grand piano to Mellotron. Kirby Gregory adds some incredibly uplifting guitar moments, before the marching beat returns to wind down the nearly ten-minute long epic. Eddie goes for a bit of ragtime piano near the end of the song. It has an almost show dance feel to it.

'World' is a very brief track; a catchy little ditty which acts as a transition between the LP's first and second sides. Like 'Metamorphosis', the instrumental 'Armin' harks back to the band's progressive rock sound. Kirby Gregory's guitar pyrotechnics add extra dimension to the track. 'U.H.F' is an atmospheric instrumental part bookended by two pieces of heavy glam rock. It delves into a hard rock style, largely due to Kirby's riffs in the first couple of minutes, changing to beautiful piano and Mellotron parts. The last two tracks very much signify the hard rock direction that is predominant on *Air Cut*; 'Two-Three-Two' and 'Easy'.

When asked his opinion of *Air Cut*, Kirby was quoted in *Guitar* in July 1973:

> It's a pretty good statement of affairs at the time, but it's out of date already, obviously, because we recorded it in January. The thing is, it's got a lot of different directions on it, which you could criticise us for. You can't listen to it and say, 'Ah, that's the direction they're going to go' – people get confused. I think we lost quite a lot of fans, but then we gained a lot of new fans who previously thought Curved Air was a middle-class rock band, if you know what I mean. I think we widened the scope of the band, but without losing anything musically. The next album will definitely be more of a band effort, not such a collection of individual ideas.

Air Cut was recorded between January and February 1973 at Advision Studios in London. It showcased the group's progressive rock and folk-orientated elements whilst being demonstrative of the willingness to go in new directions with regards to hard rock. Within the new line-up, an enthusiasm for embracing technology is there, particularly on 'Elfin Boy', where Eddie Jobson's VCS3 synthesizer and harpsichord add some chilling and spooky effects.

Although *Air Cut* was stylistically very different to Curved Air's previous albums, the same level of musical intelligence was there in terms of highly talented musicians working on getting the best sound possible with the technology available to them. Upon being asked what other electronics he used, Kirby told the following to *Guitar* in July 1973 (there's quite a bit of guitar-specific jargon here, but I think it's worth including because it is certainly a point of interest from a musician's perspective, and it's demonstrative of how much thought Kirby, and indeed all of Curved Air, put into their work):

A Dan Armstrong Green Ringer, which gives me an octave up; A Dan Armstrong treble-boost and bass-boost combined with a Cry Baby wah-wah peddle. Actually, I've got two of those because they sound different: one gives a very thin, straight wah-wah sound, and the other doesn't have so much wah-wah, but it's got a very metallic sound, full of middle. And I've got a Uni-Vibe: it's an American thing, like an electronic Leslie cabinet. I tried others, but the Uni-Vibe is the only one that's any good. Unfortunately, you can't get it in this country. Dan Armstrong has made a new guitar, you know, and he's set up his own company to distribute it. He's given me one – it's like the Dan Armstrong perspex guitar I already use but made of wood, and the pick-up is on a metal bar, so you can slide it backwards and forwards to give a big tone range. It's a double-coiled pick-up – very powerful – which gives a sound somewhat somewhere between the Fender and the Gibson. On the plexiglass guitar, I've got two different pick-ups made by Dan Armstrong, you know, they're interchangeable, you just slot them in. One is like a Fender pick-up – which I don't use much because I've got the Strat anyway – and the other is like a Gibson humbucker, but about twice as powerful. In fact, you have to be careful about what amps you use. When we made the album, I used a Fender Twin Reverb, and I blew the input stage because the output from this pick-up was so strong.

When asked in the same feature if he used the same equipment on stage as in the studio, Kirby explained:

Yes, except that in the studio, I don't use the Uni-Vibe, I use a real Leslie. But since we've got two of those for the organ, it's impractical to take one on the road for the guitar as well.

When asked if there was a musical difference between the recording studio and the stage, Kirby explained:

(There's) a world of difference. On stage, you can't afford to do things that don't sink in straight away. Audiences are attentive and they listen well, but they're not superhuman – you can't expect them to hear things that they would on record. So I go for the more basic approach on stage, I want things to be immediate. You see, I'm not just into playing guitar. The two other things I'm interested in are writing songs and entertaining people – and I don't mean I want to be an all-round entertainer! I could never be an all-round entertainer. It's all down to realising your limitations.

When *Air Cut* was released in the spring of 1973, it didn't do well commercially. The band split up as Eddie Jobson replaced Brian Eno in Roxy Music. Kirby formed Stretch with Elmer Gantry. Mike Wedgwood joined Kiki Dee's backing band – supporting Elton John on the *Goodbye Yellow Brick Road* tour – and joined Caravan from 1974 to 1976. Musically, *Air Cut* is certainly not without merit, but essentially – despite the beginnings of an attempt to make another album together – the 1973 Curved Air line-up decided to call it quits. It seems that Eddie Jobson went to Roxy Music with a sense of certainty and commitment, so much so that he was prepared to change instruments. He was quoted in *Keyboard* in November 2016: 'I had sold my first Hammond to Jon Lord of Deep Purple when I joined Roxy Music in 1973'.

Sonja Kristina asserted of *Air Cut* in *Melody Maker* in May 1973:

To be honest, it has been our most disappointing album to date. I think that the lack of interest in it has been because we could only get across to so many people on our recent tour. It's a very varied album. I mean Kirby is into blues, Eddie's into electronic things like ELP, and they had to be given the chance to feature themselves. I think the people that have listened to it are pleased with what they hear, and I'm confident about the next one … This will be a better one, it has to be.

The 1973 line-up presented plenty of talent and scope to make a worthwhile album, in the form of *Air Cut*. Sonja Kristina told *Hit Channel* in December 2018:

Darryl and Francis were opting to make their own music and also to have a rest. They were very tired, very burned out and they couldn't keep up the pace. So, I got to get a new band featuring Eddie Jobson, who had supported us when we played at Mayfair Ballroom in Newcastle with his band, Fat Grapple. He was a big fan of our band, and he knew all the songs from Curved Air and he also learned songs from a lot of other progressive rock bands. He played keyboards as well, so he was obviously the only person who was equipped to step into Darryl and Francis' shoes, as he was able to play the Curved Air songs as they had been and also to create new songs that fitted with the Curved Air roster. Then we auditioned Kirby, and I was just blown away by his sound. He had such a big, wild sound and he was a wonderful concert performer. He kept very physical and his playing was powerful. So, those two, and Jim Russell – a solid, expressive drummer – and Mike Wedgwood, who had been playing with us on *Phantasmagoria*, and he has inherited the arrangements from the old line-up to this line-up. We had the challenge to make a new album and we set about putting a couple of my songs in – 'Elfin Boy' and 'Easy' – and I wrote lyrics for the other ones. We were produced by Martin Rushent, who became a very famous producer, and he was lovely to work with. He was key in helping us develop the songs and the arrangements of those. In the first three Curved Air albums, Darryl's writing had been quite simple and lyrical, and Francis' music was much more rocky, and in terms of 'Piece Of Mind', he was very, very epic. So, we had an epic piece from Eddie with 'Metamorphosis', with rocky things from Kirby, and a violin instrumental, 'Armin'. So, it had the pillars of Curved Air success to me. I think it was more immediate; it would reach a wider audience, in a way. It had all the elements of Curved Air. I thought it had a much more immediate appeal. It was a little drama to catch on, but now it's one of the most popular Curved Air albums.

All Curved Air line-ups certainly presented as a talented and enterprising team. Martin Rushent's career credits also include working with The Stranglers and Buzzcocks. Essentially, whilst *Air Cut* wasn't particularly successful at the time of its release, the album is generally well-regarded in the context of Curved Air's long-standing discography. It was reported in *Melody Maker* in July 1973:

Curved Air have cracked down the centre for the second time in their short career. Splits hit Curved Air this week, with violinist Eddie Jobson – who replaced Darryl Way – leaving the group, along with the lead guitarist, Kirby, and Jim Russell. Air spokesman, Tony Brainsby, told the *Melody Maker*: 'Kirby and Jim are forming a new group together, details of which will be announced next week. But there is no split in Curved Air, because it will continue as a live recording band. Sonja Kristina will be getting new musicians together of her own choosing, and they will start work this week on recording a new album'. The future of Air bass guitarist Mike Wedgwood is uncertain, but he may be working with Sonja on the albums. Reasons for the split (are), 'We have no excuse to offer', said Brainsby, 'It's just a reshuffle'.

As was reported in August 1973 in the *Coventry Evening Telegraph:*

It's hard to keep up with who is and who isn't with such and such a group these days. Within a few days, Roxy Music, Family, Kinks, Curved Air, Mott The Hoople and Strawbs, have all had changes. Eno has left Roxy Music, and Eddie Jobson – violinist-guitarist of the broken up Curved Air – replaces him. Other Curved Air musicians, Jim Russell (drums) and Kirby (guitar) are forming a new group. Vocalist, Sonja Kristina, is looking for other musicians to form a new Curved Air.

It may have been the case that Sonja Kristina had the initial intention of getting a new line-up together. It didn't happen, though, and as such, Curved Air disbanded entirely before the end of 1973, not to become an active entity again until late in 1974, as the next chapter will demonstrate.

Lovechild is the band's seventh studio album. However, only half of the tracks are actually performed by the group. The album consists of previously unreleased demos made in the early-1970s; one by John O'Hara, two by Eddie Jobson, one by Kirby Gregory, and four by Curved Air. The demo tapes were made for Warner Bros., but when Clifford Davis presented the tapes to them, the record company had already decided that they didn't want to continue the Curved Air contract.

In *Record Collector* in April 2012, Sonja Kristina offered her opinion on where *Lovechild* sits in the grand scheme of the band's discography:

Those tracks were mainly demos for what was supposed to be the album after Air Cut. Eddie and Kirby had left. Also, Mike Wedgwood, the bass player since *Phantasmagoria*, was planning something with Florian, which left me on my own. They were all very supportive, though I was also trying to pull in other players, like Jerry Goodman (from Flock) and Jon Lord (from Deep Purple). When those songs were issued in 1990, they came with outtakes that had nothing or little to do with me. 'Joan', for example, was a song Eddie and I had been working on, but the instrumental version on *Lovechild* was stuck on, along with other rough outtakes that had more to do with Stretch or Eddie than Curved Air.

The *Lovechild* tracks are predominantly made up of demos. Sonja Kristina seemed keen to distance herself from the project. She did, however, say of the track, 'Seasons', in *The Arts Desk* in April 2014:

> The lyrics are nice. It's not something I'd want to do now because it's too static, though maybe it would work with more stripped-down music, just keyboards or something to give it room to breathe.

As was perhaps implied in Sonja's comment, *Lovechild* is ultimately (what could be argued as being) an official bootleg. Neither Warner Bros. nor any of the band members gave permission for the demos to be released, and no sales royalties were paid to any of the members. However, years after the album's initial release, Repertoire Records obtained permission from both Warner Bros. and the musicians to reissue *Lovechild*, and in 2011, an approved version with new liner notes was released. Unlike the original album release, it was only available in CD format.

The four Curved Air demos were recorded between *Air Cut* and the band's breakup. Jim Russell and Kirby Gregory had already left, replaced on the demos by Florian Pilkington-Miksa, and Icelandic guitarist, Thordur Arnason, known to the other band members as simply Thor. The album's cover is simply the *Air Conditioning* front cover superimposed over the same album's back cover artwork.

By 1973, Curved Air were not in a stable position financially. In *Melody Maker* in May 1973, Sonja Kristina surmised the situation:

> If you mean, am I financially secure, then the answer is no. I'd like to be, because then I'd be able to help the band with equipment and things. Curved Air is far from being broke, it's made a lot of money, but most of it was chewed up as the band became more popular. Musically, I'm very happy with the way things have turned out. True, the first album sold more than any of the others, but the development of the band has been so great music-wise, that it's been rewarding.

It was this lack of financial stability that would largely inform what was to happen in 1974.

1974

Whilst away from Curved Air in 1973, Darryl Way formed his new band, Wolf. The line-up included fusion guitarist John Etheridge (later to join Soft Machine), bassist and vocalist, Dek Messecar (later to join Caravan), and drummer extraordinaire Ian Mosley (later of Trace and then Marillion). This line-up of Wolf recorded two albums. The first, *Canis Lupis* – released in 1973 – was produced by King Crimson virtuoso Ian McDonald.

Record Mirror reviewed Wolf's debut album in March 1973:

Darryl Way (ex-Curved Air) and his new lads. A good production, with cascading chords early on, some pleasantly languid vocal touches in between the odd lash of percussion and drive. It's not one of yer instant hit touches, but it's got a fair amount of fascination inbuilt. At least try it.

Note how often it was the case that the media felt the need to mention that Darryl Way was a former Curved Air member.

The second album, *Saturation Point*, was also released in 1973. Wolf also recorded three non-album singles – 'Spring Fever', 'Five In The Morning' and 'A Bunch Of Fives' – and performed a live concert for the BBC at the Paris Theatre in London.

An early Wolf performance (along with Greenslade) was reviewed in *Record Mirror* in February 1973:

It was a strange bit of planning, having two new bands making their debut on the same bill, let alone putting both fledgelings into a speedily-collapsing nest. Thursday's double-first took place on the last night at Mile End, Sundown. And it was very evidently the end of Mile End – half the staff seemed to think it had already closed, which resulted in a long wait before anyone could be found to open a bar for road-weary journalists. And so to the music. Darryl Way's new group, Wolf, were the headliners and did enough to suggest a fairly bright future. They had a little too much crescendo and climax for my liking, but there was plenty of spirit and professionalism and a fair amount of flash in evidence. Which, apart from a few flashes of Vivaldi on Darryl's violin, was about the only genuine similarity with Curved Air. One of the quarter passages had a couple of boppers waltzing front-stage, which makes a nice change from idiot dancers. Surprisingly, Darryl spent much of his time on keyboards, often leaving the limelight to a very original guitarist, John Etheridge.

As well as having the attention of an international audience, Wolf were keenly anticipated by the media, as was the case in *Record Mirror* in August 1973 under the heading of 'Wolf On The Way':

Darryl Way's Wolf will make a British and European tour to coincide with their second album release in October. Over the next three weeks, they will record the entirely instrumental LP. They leave for concerts and TV in Germany, Holland and France on August 20, returning on September 12 to finish the album. Their tour starts on October 7 at Birmingham Town Hall and ends at Manchester Free Trade Hall on 31. They will play The Rainbow and 20 more venues yet to be announced.

In 1974, vocalist John Hodkinson was added to the group and Wolf recorded their next album, *Night Music*: an album indicative of Wolf's musical potential. In particular, the opening track – 'The Envoy' – features strong musicianship weaved into a piece that showcases some distinctively memorable melodies.

But even by midway into 1974, Way was looking to form a new band, with the assistance of his manager at the time, Miles Copeland III. Miles recommended his brother Stewart Copeland as a drummer, and the band played several gigs under the name Stark Naked And The Car Thieves. In an interview with *Music Street Journal* in October 2013, Darryl Way recalled the time when he fell through a hole in the stage at a Wolf gig. His violin got smashed up and he only had his perspex violin as backup:

It wouldn't have been too bad, but for the fact that the whole Wolf set was played using viola tuning (a fifth lower than a violin) and I didn't have any spare viola strings. Therefore I had to tune the violin strings down a fifth, which made the violin sound like a bee in a jam jar and also made it impossible to keep in tune. By the end of the gig, there were only two people left in the hall. It wouldn't have been so bad, except for the fact that Miles Copeland had come especially to see us that night with a view to managing us. Needless to say, he wasn't too impressed, but eventually, he did end up managing me.

Sonja Kristina briefly returned to *Hair* for three months in the summer of 1974. It seems that her affinity with the musical was such that it was a natural decision for her. She told *Melody Maker* in May 1973:

> I'd love to get into acting. I've always been interested in theatre. I might go into something like another production of *Hair* or do films. I said when we formed the new band, that I wanted to be free to do things as an individual. I think it'll help the band a lot, because they'll be free to do whatever they want to do. It should keep frustrations away. I'm learning to play an assortment of musical instruments, so that I can play on stage. I want to be considered as a musician, although the rest of the band aren't too keen on the idea. They think it'll ruin my image.

It wasn't long after, that a financial crisis emerged for the original Curved Air band members. They owed significant back taxes and were being sued by Chrysalis for defaulting on their contract. In order to cover the debts, Darryl Way, Francis Monkman and Florian Pilkington-Miksa – along with new member, American bassist, Phil Kohn – reunited for a UK tour in December of 1974. Kohn played on the reunion tour and appeared on the *Curved Air Live* album. He stayed with the band following the tour and participated in the first (although aborted!) recording sessions for what was to become the *Midnight Wire* album. He toured extensively with the new version of Curved Air, and his bass can be heard on the 1975 Curved Air BBC transcription disk.

Phil Kohn's audition was an interesting one. When it was his turn to play with the band, Darryl Way told him that he'd had enough of playing the same stuff over and over again for audition purposes, and could Phil please suggest something different. Cue a jazz improvisation: it impressed the band and Kohn was put on the payroll. Being from L.A., Kohn wasn't particularly familiar with Curved Air or their music. During two weeks of rehearsals at Covent Garden prior to the start of the reunion tour, the rest of the band had played the songs many times and therefore spent more time drinking tea than practising. Kohn was struggling to memorise the music and grew quite nervous about it to the extent that he had prepared cheat sheets that he hoped to be able to conceal on stage. No chance though! On the night of the first gig, he found out just how big Curved Air were in the UK, and was surprised by the scale of the arena, the stage and the roadies. Everything turned out fine. Such was the extent to which Curved Air attracted musicians rather than stars perhaps.

Finance was a powerful motivator behind the brief 1974 reformation of the first Curved Air line-up. When asked about it in an interview with *Record Collector* in April 2012, Sonja Kristina candidly replied:

It came when my personal life was in chaos, which is reflected, I suppose, in my raw delivery on the consequent live album. Also, I wore jewelled G-strings and ragged see-through lace dresses with feathers and tassels – the result perhaps of months of Playboy culture. A feeling of nonchalant abandon certainly influenced the way I dressed and behaved on stage. In any case, I've always preferred performing to the studio, where you have to adhere to the way the writer has perceived a particular item. When you're doing it onstage, however, there are no such restrictions. It is shamanistic direct communication.

Although there was perhaps a sense of obligation behind Curved Air's late-1974 reunion tour, it seems that it was met with enthusiasm by both the fans and the media, even if there was some cynicism present about how long the band would last. As was reported in *The Liverpool Echo* on Friday 1 November 1974:

The original reformed Curved Air – Sonja Kristina, Darryl Way, Francis Monkman and Florian Pilkington-Miksa – with the addition of American bass player Phil Kohn, play Liverpool Stadium on November 24 as part of their one-off national tour. After the tour, the band are expected to disband again.

It was reported in *The Newcastle Journal* in November 1974:

One of Mayfair's most popular acts makes a return to the scene of former triumph tonight. Curved Air is a band in business, having reformed their original line-up after a split which did none of them much good. Now, demon violinist Darryl Way is back in action with singer Sonja Kristina and company at the ballroom which always gave them a good reception.

When Curved Air were due to perform at Hastings Pier, journalist Stephen Turner, had great enthusiasm for the band's line-up as it was in November 1974:

Remember 'Back Street Luv'? Well, even if you don't, the reformed Curved Air are still worth a trip to the Pier on Saturday. The original line-up split some time ago, and a weakened revived version did not last long either. However, last month they got together again and began a massive tour with all the original line-up, with the exception of new bassist Phil Kohn.

It is interesting how Turner seems to minimise the achievements of one line-up in comparison to Curved Air's original one. Without the line-up that Turner negates, the *Air Cut* album wouldn't exist as it is.

1975

Curved Air – Live

Personnel:
Sonja Kristina: lead vocals
Darryl Way: violin, keyboards, backing vocals
Francis Monkman: lead guitar, organ, VCS3 synthesizer
Florian Pilkington-Miksa: percussion
Philip Kohn: bass guitar
Design and Artwork: Liz Gilmore
Photography: Michael Allard for BTM design
Recorded live at Cardiff University and Bristol Polytechnic in December 1974 with the Manor Mobile
Producer: David Hitchcock for BTM Productions
Re-mixed at Air Studios, London
Engineer and Re-mix engineer: Django Johnny Punter
Assistant Engineers: Phil Becque, Paul Nunn, Sean Milligan, Andy Morris and Alan Perkins
Highest chart positions: Did not chart
Side one: 1. 'It Happened Today' 5:25, 2. 'Marie Antoinette' 6:45, 3. 'Back Street Luv' 3:43, 4. 'Propositions' 7:42
Side two: 5. 'Young Mother' 8:56, 6. 'Vivaldi' 9:00, 7. 'Everdance' 5:36

Midnight Wire (1975)

Personnel:
Sonja Kristina: lead vocals
Darryl Way: violin
Mick Jacques: guitars
Stewart Copeland: drums
John G. Perry: bass guitar
Peter Wood: keyboards
Derek Damain: backing vocals (3)
Engineer: Will Reid-Dick
Sleeve design: Bob Searles and Liz Gilmore
Studio: Ramport Studios, London
Producers: Ron and Howard Albert for FAT Productions
Highest chart positions: Did not chart
Side one: 1. 'Woman On A One Night Stand' (Sonja Kristina, Norma Tager) 5:06, 2. 'Day Breaks My Heart' (Darryl Way, Tager) 4:38, 3. 'The Fool' (Way,

Mick Jacques, Tager) 4:27, 4. 'Pipe Of Dreams' (Jacques) 3:58
Side two 5. 'Orange Street Blues' (Way, Tager) 5:01 6. 'Dance Of Love'
(Jacques, Way, Tager) 4:36 7. 'Midnight Wire' (Way, Tager) 7:32

Curved Air Live was recorded during an intensive three week UK tour
and featured strong versions of some of the band's stage favourites:
'Vivaldi' (with an added vocal section and highland fling), 'Back Street
Luv', 'Young Mother' and an extended version of 'Propositions'. A
live single – featuring 'It Happened Today' and 'Back Street Luv' – was
issued, but it didn't do much commercially. Perhaps the media felt
that there wasn't much to say about it. In April 1975, the *Thanet Times*
said of the live single 'Back Street Luv'/'It Happened Today': 'Live
recordings of the group's most famous singles taken from the new
concert album'.

After the tour, and with financial debts settled, Francis Monkman
went off to form Sky, and Florian Pilkington-Miksa drifted out of the
music scene. Darryl Way permanently disbanded Wolf and formed a
new version of Curved Air with Sonja Kristina. Darryl did not cut all ties
with Wolf, though, playing with bandmate Ian Mosley on the 1975 Trace
album, *Birds*. *Curved Air Live* was reviewed in *Cash Box* in May 1975:

Curved Air is another space-rock group from England, coming to the
shores of America. Sounding like Yes, Genesis and Pink Floyd, this
group, however, does indeed have its own flavour due to the electrifying
violin work of Darryl Way. Combining elements of classical with rock is
becoming ever more popular across the country, and the work on this
live album makes this an exciting and enjoyable listening album. The
five-piece Curved Air band work well together, playing off each other to
create an interesting musical experience in cuts like 'It Happened Today',
'Back Street Luv', 'Young Mother' and 'Everdance'.

The new line-up toured extensively throughout 1975 and began to
redevelop their sound and thus, their fanbase. This was reported in the
Reading Evening Post under the title, 'Curved Air Stage Comeback' in
February 1975:

The gamble is paying off; Curved Air can still make it after two years
of lying dormant. Their November-December tour with the original

line-up had halls packed with nostalgic fans, and their current tour is strengthening their position. At Reading University, they received encores from an exuberant rag-week audience, who staggered back to their halls of residence to dream of delicious Sonja Kristina. She slinks around the stage, her slender body moving like a leaf in the wind to the strains of Darryl Way's violin. Curved Air vintage 1975 is a lot heavier than Curved Air vintage 1970. Keyboards are pretty much absent and Sonja's voice has a rougher quality. The whole band has more of a rock feel to it.

The Newcastle Journal reported on Friday 21 February 1975:

Tonight the city hall plays host to a band that always had a big following in this area: Curved Air, which has been resurrected after a two-year break. Darryl Way and singer Sonja Kristina were sufficiently encouraged by the success of last year's temporary reunion to form a new line-up, and this is their first tour.

The bands on the bill that night offered something of interest for music fans that embraced a nod to classical music. Also due to perform was a new Dutch trio called Trace. The band was set up by the award-winning pianist, Rick van der Linden, who was previously the leader of Ekseption (a band very much worth looking up if you like Curved Air – Ekseption did a fascinating version of Bach's *Toccata And Fugue* on their 1973 album, *Trinity*).

The 1975 line-up retained Sonja Kristina and Darryl Way, whilst welcoming newcomers Mick Jacques (on guitar), major guest player John Perry (on bass) and twenty-two-year-old drummer Stewart Copeland. Jacques had previously worked with Copeland in the band Cat Iron. 1975 was the year Curved Air recorded and released the album *Midnight Wire*. Stewart Copeland briefly worked as the band's manager but found it difficult to work with Darryl in a business situation compared to a creative one. Even so, it was during this time that Copeland's relationship with Sonja Kristina evolved, and they were soon living together in the first of a series of flats throughout London. Sonja was eventually to marry Stewart Copeland. Upon being asked if their relationship was a source of friction within the band, Sonja told *Prog* in February 2018:

I think the guys in the band had already gotten used to me being involved with someone from a touring party. Before we released our debut album, *Air Conditioning*, Curved Air toured with Black Sabbath, and I had a relationship with their manager, Malcolm Ross. Everyone was very cool about that, and there was never a sign of friction, so when Stewart and I got together, I never expected any problems. And there were none. Besides, the boys were busy hanging out with girls, so they had their own situations to deal with.

John Perry's time with Curved Air was brief. When he had left Caravan, Mike Wedgwood had just left Curved Air to *join* Caravan. Caravan had recently moved to Curved Air's management. With that band being about to get back together again to record an album, Perry was asked to join – just to play on the one album, and one gig at the Isle of Man.

Mick Jacques played on tour with the band and appeared on *Midnight Wire*, *Airborne*, and *Live At The BBC*. Jacques contributed the stunning instrumental, 'Pipe Of Dreams', as well as co-writing the tracks 'Stark Naked', 'The Fool', 'Dance Of Love', 'Desiree', 'Touch Of Tequila' and 'Hot And Bothered'.

Sonja Kristina's friend, Norma Tager – who had helped design Sonja's onstage costumes, from Curved Air's 1974 reunion to their breakup in 1976 – contributed all of the song lyrics on *Midnight Wire*.

Midnight Wire received a mixed reception from both fans and Curved Air members. It seems that by 1975, the band were in tumultuous times; the live shows in 1974 had been predominantly about sorting a financial problem, and artistically, it is probable that everyone was just going though the motions. On the other hand, there is no denying that the new line-up had much to offer, and in light of that, to dismiss *Midnight Wire* as being absent of any musical interest, would certainly be flawed. Certainly, Darryl Way was still proactive in wanting to get the best out of the technology available when it came to thinking about innovative ways to get a good sound. *International Musician & Recording World* reported in March 1975:

Darryl Way, violinist with Curved Air, has managed to solve a problem caused by his perspex violin. Although the violin had good visual appearance, the dense body caused harshness of tone. Now Darryl has taken delivery of a Yamaha RA 100 rotary tone cabinet, which he uses for his violin. He has also added a Yamaha RA 100 to his Fender Piano and Yamaha Synthesizer setup.

1973's *Air Cut* had already been demonstrative of the fact that, stylistically, Curved Air could and indeed did change. By the time *Midnight Wire* came along, perhaps keeping an open mind would have been the way forward for the band and their fans. Although the band had been dropped by Warner Bros., they had found a new record company to represent them. It was announced in *Billboard* in March 1975:

> A new label for RCA, BTM (British Talent Management) with a first release of the Renaissance album, *Turn Of The Cards*. Future signings to the label will include Caravan, Curved Air, Climax Blues Band, American Gypsy and Sonja Kristina.

Record Mirror & Disc reported in October 1975 that Curved Air would be going on the road to do talk shows in order to publicise the *Midnight Wire* album. They were given the midnight slot on local radio stations. The idea came about from a successful Capitol Radio show the band had done earlier that year.

Although *Midnight Wire* was a change in musical direction, the album offers an interesting style of pop/rock that, in parts, features a lot of romantic guitar and violin interplay. Equally, there are plenty of aspects that veer towards heavy rock, yet not quite to the extent of entering the power ballad territory.

On the opening track – 'Woman On A One Night Stand' – Sonja Kristina's vocals are hyper-expressive. 'Day Breaks My Heart' has a compelling jazzy style, and 'The Fool' has some funky rhythms. As much as a stylistic change was present, the album was certainly not without elements that harked back to the earlier Curved Air sound. 'Pipe Of Dreams' is a very atmospheric track, with the violin providing plenty of interest. An instrumental, 'Pipe Of Dreams' is still reflective of a group of musicians willing to explore interesting territory. The general mood of *Midnight Wire* seems quite blues-based: for instance, the track 'Orange Street Blues'. Equally, 'Dance Of Love' has a soul flavour to it. The last song – the album's title track – is poppy and lilting with an almost sentimental guitar solo.

With Darryl Way back in the fold for *Midnight Wire*, the album probably benefitted from his compositional input. But it may have been the case that in terms of the album overall, Francis Monkman's influence was perhaps the missing ingredient in comparison to the band's earlier albums. That's not to say there was a lack of talent present on *Midnight*

Wire, not at all! But the fact is that, stylistically, the Curved Air writing team had changed considerably by 1975. Musically, the album does have a lot to offer, but commercially, one of the factors that perhaps made it struggle at the time, could have been that it was just so different to what people might have expected from Curved Air.

It is understandable why some may consider *Midnight Wire* to show a perhaps somewhat disappointing change in direction; Curved Air had made their name in the early 1970s as a progressive rock band. The apparent rejection of that style on *Midnight Wire* – in favour of something more rock and blues-rock-based – is possibly something that not many fans were happy about. I would suggest that to get the best out of *Midnight Wire*, it's best to embrace it as something that stands in its own right. Importantly though, Sonja Kristina wasn't too pleased with the album and, on such basis, it is understandable that her creative mind may have started wandering towards other career options then. She told *Prog* in February 2018:

When we did the albums *Midnight Wire* and *Airborne*, I wasn't at all happy with the musical direction the band were going in. Sure, we were getting a very strong reaction from the fans, who were going wild for us. But I was totally unmoved. I was dissatisfied with what we were doing. The original line-up had been technically superb but also very exciting. But in that era, Darryl was taking us into a much more blues-rock and pop-oriented approach, and that didn't appeal to me. Sure, the musicians we had at the time were very gifted, and you cannot argue with what they brought to Curved Air. But I felt removed from it all. I was going through the motions and did think about leaving to start my own band. The way Curved Air was heading, wasn't for me.

In some of the periods away from Curved Air, Sonja worked in a colourful array of employments, including being a clerk and a croupier. It could perhaps be said that in the year prior to *Midnight Wire* being made, a lot had gone on that had put morale in a state of fine balance. Sonja Kristina told *Record Collector* in April 2012:

Warners had not taken up the option of another album (after *Air Cut*, all subsequent albums were on the BTM label). All the money was handled by management, and so funding stopped. After nine months of dealing cards night after night at the Playboy Club, I was back in *Hair*. It was a short run, but others from the 1968 team were there too. Around that time, pre-punk cynicism was creeping in, and I remember doing a solo college tour with Country Joe, and even he was sceptical about the hippie dream. However, I was still convinced that the movement had opened doors, particularly as the cross-pollination of artistic genres and the awakening of eastern and western spiritual practices – yoga, vegetarianism, meditation and so forth – were becoming mainstream by then. Around that time, I became friends with Norma Tager, and because I felt then that I hadn't much to say as far as lyrics were concerned, she stepped into the breach after I taught her the basic principles of songwriting. Though the lyrics on *Midnight Wire* are attributed to Norma, they were her version of what I was going through emotionally when my marriage to Malcolm was breaking up. The original master of *Midnight Wire*, which was fantastic, was rejected by the company. That version has disappeared. Instead, what was very adventurous material was watered down to something more in tune with the conventions of the day. We had a terrible time, especially Stewart, who was told to go away and practice with a metronome.

The *Reading Evening Post* reviewed *Midnight Wire* in December 1975:

Once upon a time, Curved Air might have had a lot to say, but that time has passed. Now all they are doing is providing pretty little songs in a singer-and-backing-band role. And Sonja Kristina, sexy lady though she is, doesn't have a strong enough voice to carry it off. They're just not punchy enough, although there's a hint of the power that they're capable of. Perhaps it will return in time.

1976

Airborne

Personnel:
Sonja Kristina: vocals
Darryl Way: violin, keyboards
Tony Reeves: bass, keyboards, double bass (3)
Stewart Copeland: drums
Mick Jacques: guitars
Robin Lumley: piano (3)
Alan Skidmore: saxophone on (8)
Henry Lowther: trumpet on (8)
Frank Ricotti: congas
Jack Emblow: accordion on (3)
Bob Sargeant: organ on (1) and (2)
Studio: Trident Studio, London
Producers: Dennis McKay (3-5, 7, and 8) and Curved Air (1, 2, 6, and 9)
Highest chart places: did not chart
Side one: 1. 'Desiree' (Stewart Copeland, Sonja Kristina, Mick Jacques)
3:12, 2. 'Kids To Blame' (Norma Tager, Copeland) 3:19, 3. 'Broken Lady'
(Kristina, Tony Reeves) 3:13, 4. 'Juno' (Darryl Way) 3:23, 5. 'Touch Of
Tequila' (Kristina, Jacques, Reeves) 3:49
Side two: 6. 'Moonshine' (Way) 11:36, 7. 'Heaven (Never Seemed So
Far Away)' (Copeland, Stuart Lyons) 3:18, 8. 'Hot And Bothered' (Tager,
Jacques) 2:53, 9. 'Dazed' (Way) 4:17

As ever, Sonja Kristina dressed in her own – often customised – style, as
was reported in the *Acton Gazette And Post* in April 1976:

The Contessa Krysha Tyszkova – Sallie to her friends – is one of the
most exuberant characters I have met in a long time. At just 27, she has
designed clothes for Mick Jagger, Rod Stewart, Twiggy and a whole host
of other personalities … Sallie's latest commission is to design an erotic
outfit for Sonja Kristina, famous for her work with the group Curved Air.
The dress will be featured on Sonja's new album cover to be released
shortly. She specialises in using pure silks, satins, hand embroidery and
appliqué. When she goes to buy some silk, she finds constant amusement
in watching the shopkeepers as she carries out her 'silk test': that is,
holding the silk before her face and blowing softly to see if it is floaty.

By the mid-1970s, after *Air Cut*, Curved Air's sound and image had changed. As part of that, Sonja Kristina's singing was less ethereal on both *Midnight Wire* and their album recorded and released in 1976, *Airborne*. She told *The Arts Desk* in April 2014:

I'd heard Janis Joplin for the first time when we were in America and was very moved by her – I don't know if that was an influence. I went through some personal problems at that time. Between *Air Cut* and the live album, my marriage to Mal Ross, who used to be Black Sabbath's tour manager, broke up, so I was going out and partying a lot and drowning my sorrows with various kinds of inebriation. The original Curved Air members had gone off to do their own things. Then I got the *Air Cut* band together and they went off, too, which left just me. I did some recordings that were apparently turned down by the record company, and the management cut off my money. I had a son to support, so I went out to work and got a job dealing cards in the Playboy Club. I ended up back in the same Hampstead flat where I used to live with the original Curved Air. I was living with this lady, Norma Tager, who ended up writing the lyrics because I just didn't want to write anything. I was drinking before the shows we did then and would be wired. I went for it with abandon, which I hadn't done before. Because I'd worked at the Playboy Club, I didn't see anything wrong with going on stage almost naked, slightly veiled with a bit of lace and stuff. I had never been so overtly feminine with Curved Air in the past. I was a kind of space gypsy, something from somewhere out there, not like a normal showgirl. We had fun buying fabrics from the market, and making new costumes, to create this glamorous, ragged, tatty look. The clothes I wear now are just a more mature version of that. I don't know if Marvel Comics' Red Sonja came out of that image, but I remember the artist (Barry Windsor-Smith) being in our dressing room at the Roundhouse one time and that I left him a note.

The 1976 *Airborne* album was pretty much Curved Air's 1970s swansong. The band line-up saw the addition of former Greenslade bassist and keyboardist Tony Reeves. Reeves was invited to join Curved Air when John Perry left following the BTM *Midnight Wire* re-recording sessions. Tony toured with the band and appeared on the *Airborne* and *Live At The BBC* recordings. He co-wrote 'Broken Lady' and 'Touch Of Tequila'. As with *Midnight Wire*, Norma Tager contributed lyrics. The *Airborne* album sessions document the debut of Stewart Copeland as a songwriter. Around the release of *Midnight Wire*, he was told about publishing royalties for songwriters. He responded by churning out compositions until the band accepted some of his contributions.

In an interview with *Home & Studio Recording* in December 1983, Stewart Copeland explained how he managed his contract with Curved Air from a writing perspective:

> The band had negotiated a deal with Island Publishing, whereby they paid an advance to the group and the whole group signed up as songwriters. But I held out, I thought, 'Well, wait a minute, if I sign this deal, the advance is going to go to the two songwriters of the group, Sonja Kristina and Darryl Way, they will take it all, so what have I got to gain by signing this deal'. So I held out, I refused to sign, and so Island said, 'OK, well if you can write one song on the next album, we'll give you a £750 advance'. I had millions of riffs and motifs, atmospheres, grooves and stuff which I'd try and play to the band in the hope that they'd accept one of them for the album, but I'd forgotten which notes they were by then, anyway, and so I couldn't show them how to do it! My songs all depended on recording technique – they were not really band material. I still suffer from that problem incidentally, which is why I've been saved by film scores, as you only need 30-second ideas, but lots of them. You don't have to develop ideas; you don't have to find a verse or shape it into the pop song format. Anyhow, I managed to write a song and get it on the album and figured out the chords to show the guitarist how he should play it, and I got the £750.

Essentially, had Copeland not had a good business head on him, the content on *Airborne* could have been considerably different. He has writing credits on the tracks, 'Desiree', 'Kids To Blame' and 'Heaven (Never Seemed So Far Away)'. Sonja Kristina said of 'Desiree' in *Record Collector* in April 2012: 'It came out as a single. To me, it's reminiscent now of the early Police, and it was, essentially, Stewart's song.'

The Police covered 'Kids To Blame' in their early performances. Their take of the song is structurally simpler than Curved Air's version and is played in a punk style. Stewart Copeland also re-used a guitar riff from 'Desiree' in his solo single as Klark Kent: 'Don't Care'.

As had been the case during the recording of *Midnight Wire*, *Airborne* was plagued by difficulties with producers. Producer, Dennis McKay, quit the project midway through recording, which left the remaining four tracks to be produced by Curved Air themselves. The disruptive working process ended up costing Curved Air large sums of money by putting them back in debt to their record company. Curved Air's popularity as a live band could only keep them going for so long, especially due to the fact that punk rock was beginning to dominate the music scene, and interest in progressive acts was continuing to diminish. *Airborne* was not a significant commercial success. After a follow-up non-album single – 'Baby Please Don't Go' (with 'Broken Lady' on the B-side) – the group disbanded. Of the single, *Record Mirror* considered in November 1976: 'Blues oldie rocks again just like the Them version'.

On Curved Air's performance at Cardiff Castle, *Record Mirror* asserted in July 1976:

> Curved Air still have their fans and found some new ones on Saturday. Sonja Kristina caused some heart-fluttering with her revealing stage costume, and when they moved into long instrumentals, they showed they could boogie with the best of them.

Curved Air spent much of their last active 1970s year on the road but still managed to find time to record *Airborne*. Although commercially, it pretty much passed unnoticed at the time, it is still worth a listen. It is dominated by Sonja Kristina's vocals, but understandably so, in light of the fact that the album overall was more pop-orientated. 'Desiree' was chosen as a single, but again, it made little impact commercially.

Although *Airborne* is perhaps representative of Curved Air's declining years in terms of success and popularity, it still holds historic significance, as it was the band's last official studio album for decades to come.

The three Darryl Way tracks ('Juno', 'Moonshine' and 'Dazed') on the album, still do make some reference to the band's progressive rock roots. In particular, 'Moonshine': the track runs to about ten minutes and is an innovative piece. The tempo and mood change throughout, whereby it moves from soft, delicate passages to Way's trademark virtuoso violin. It also features some interesting use of symphonic keyboards.

Side one consists of five short tracks. 'Desiree' is a pop-rock opener. It features multi-tracked vocals by Sonja, and some notable, if brief, lead guitar. Sonja's multi-tracked voice is apparent on several tracks. 'Kids To Blame' is pretty much a pop rock piece. That is not to say, though, that a lack of musical complexity makes the song poorer for it. Side one's closing track, 'Touch Of Tequila', could be thought of as being the antithesis of 'Moonshine', in that it is very much a pop-influenced song. 'Broken Lady', co-written by Sonja Kristina, and Darryl Way's lullaby 'Dazed' which closes the album, are both worthwhile ballads.

The *Thanet Times* reviewed *Airborne* in July 1976:

> Listening to the album, it is clear that the group has now grown into a tight band of much ability. Sonja Kristina's voice can easily be recognised and is sounding better than ever. The album opens with a typical Curved Air song, 'Desiree', and continues in fine fashion through nine inventive tracks, to end with 'Dazed' and some nice synthesizer lines.

Essentially, the *Airborne* album really is such an eclectic mix of ideas and musical styles that its scope spans progressive rock and pop. It could be said that the album is very much of its time; a time that, in hindsight, was the beginning of the gradual decline in interest in progressive rock (at least in the mainstream!).

Airborne is very much reflective of what was almost a universal move in the progressive rock genre: towards a more streamlined and commercial sound while still holding on to a few classic characteristics. Most of the *Airborne* tracks are indeed more commercially-oriented than what had gone before, but that doesn't make it a poor album. *Airborne* was perhaps not to the liking of some purely on the basis that it diverted so much from Curved Air's earlier albums. *Airborne* was reviewed in the *Acton Gazette* in July 1976:

> Curved Air is one of those frustrating groups who have promised so much yet somehow never really delivered the goods. When they first burst into life in 1970 with their *Air Conditioning* album, they had all the signs of becoming a great new talent. Their music was fresh and exciting, and Darryl Way's brash use of the violin and unprecedented adaptation of Vivaldi into a rock context, created great interest and critical acclaim. But somewhere along the line, everything started turning sour. Personnel changes started to wreck the band, and when Way eventually left in 1972, the heart fell out of their music. Sole founder-member – the gorgeous Sonja Kristina – tried to keep things going for a year, but the band's eventual death was really only a matter of time. Then, in 1974, they decided to give it one more try, and now Sonja and Darryl Way are reunited under the name of Curved Air once again. Unfortunately,

Airborne has little of the exciting originality of the early Curved Air, and Way's dynamic talents at the violin are sadly underused. I feel Ms Kristina still sings as sweet as she looks, but the album's material, in general, is rather mundane and uninspired. Just as before, Curved Air are promising much, but what they actually have to offer isn't really up to scratch.

Across each of the band's line-ups, technology was always at the forefront, as each musician strived to expand their options via the medium. In August 1976, bass and keyboard player Tony Reeves explained to *Melody Maker* what Dick Parmee – technical wizard behind Pace amplification manufacturers – was currently working on:

I came across Pace for the first time when I went to an equipment exhibition in Bloomsbury. I got interested when I found they were so well made, and I became friendly with Dick and became even more impressed with his stuff when I realised what he was doing with the standard of manufacture, design and so on. Dick is a genius at electronics, and we began talking about getting a transistor amp to sound like its valve counterpart. That's where it all starts, really, the old tranny valve controversy. In the early days of transistors, there was a lack of frontal attack in your instrument amplified through such a stack because of the slow rise-time in transistors. That's a whole lot better now because the design is better, but will still have the sound quality question. Every electronic device has distortion, and it's the type of distortion which gives an amp its characteristic sound. The valve distorts on the even-numbered harmonics and the transistor on the odd. And for some reason, to even sound better to the human – don't ask me why, it's just one of those things. Dick decided to synthesize the valve sound by the way he designed a transistor amp. He wasn't unique in wanting to do this, but I think he is the only person to have succeeded. What I'm going to have from Dick is an amp with a set of five pre-set rocker switches, and these will give me a Fender amp sound, a Fender Champ – for which Dick has even built in the sound of the little speaker – a Marshall, Hiwatt and Vox AC30. Dick has managed to achieve this by studying what it is about the circuitry of these amps that gives them their characteristic sound and reproducing it with his own design of circuit. You could have any amp sound whatsoever, provided you gave Dick enough time to check it out. The application of such a versatile setup would mainly be in the studio. I realise that most people have only one amp that they usually arrive at by trial and error. However, when recording, there are occasions where you will want a particular sound, and this is where Dick's amp would come in.

Reeves continued in the same feature:

There are two separate inputs with volume, bass, middle, treble and presence controls, of course, but the interesting part is on the right of the amp. There I've asked Dick to install all the toys you usually have on the floor. All these are built into the amp itself. The phaser unit I'm having is better, in my opinion, than the MXR, which is pretty good in itself but has been designed to withstand being kicked around since it's a foot pedal. The one thing being installed into the amp would be designed up to studio standard. There's also a noise gate, which automatically comes into operation when the phaser's being used, to cut out all the unnecessary fizzing and whining. It can be used on its own to remove all those fingering noises on the strings, and it can be inverted to introduce even more distortion and dirt with the phaser. The setup includes a limiter and compressor, for obvious reasons, a straightforward tremolo unit, and a comprehensive fuzz unit. I did toy with a digital delay line, but it may be too expensive to do. All the controls will be mounted on the panel, with just a small multicore connected up to a series of foot buttons. Oh, I almost forgot the octivider, which will go up and down, and also up and down together in whatever phase you choose. The power section will be two separate 150 watt power amps, of a completely splendid design, I hasten to add. Dick improved on power amps while he was waiting to sit an exam. He poked about in a few examples and decided he could do better, which he's done. The question of when we can get the amp on the market, is in Pace's hands, really. They've had a stupid amount of success with their nifty twelve-into-two desks. But I think Dick should get a prototype together in between six and twelve weeks.

The above information may be too technical for some people's tastes, but I have included it here because it shows the extent to which all Curved Air line-ups were active in innovation; it was the case in the earlier days of the band when they were doing well commercially, and it was the case right up until they broke up entirely in 1976 for the rest of the 1970s.

When it came to the promotional activity for *Airborne*, it was perhaps hoped that Curved Air's previous success would have been effective in encouraging sales. In the music newspapers at the time, the advert placed for *Airborne* stated:

> When the media makes this kind of exciting comment about a band, they've got to be on to something – 'Musical courage and discretion, fresh and challenging, provocative but subtle, bordered on genius' – Now they've crossed that border with their new album, *Airborne*. Surprise yourself. Get *Airborne*.

The trouble with this sort of promotion of course, is that it likely referred to Curved Air's earlier work; different music by a different line-up. A risky promotion strategy, all things considered.

It was on 25 September, while in Newcastle, that Stewart Copeland and Sonja Kristina met up with Phil Sutcliffe: a reporter who wanted them to see a favourite local act, Last Exit. Copeland saw the band's bassist and singer, Sting, as just the person he needed to launch a new band with; a band that would go on to capitalise on the rising punk and new wave phenomenon. Curved Air soon officially disbanded, at least for the remainder of the 1970s.

Darryl Way had left to go solo before *Airborne* was released. Alex Richman (ex-Butts Band) became the final member to be recruited to Curved Air, but by then, it seems the writing was already on the wall, and most members of the band perhaps felt that they were flogging a dead horse. Sonja Kristina told *Record Collector* in April 2012:

> Darryl had quit shortly before we disbanded in 1976, and Alex Richman from (The Doors' – John Densmore and Robbie Krieger's) the Butts Band, stepped in. At that point, I wanted to leave, as well. But it was only Stewart – my future husband – being in the band that kept me going. I was restless. Everybody was coming up with nice songs, but we were becoming disparate stylistically. For instance, Mick Jacques, our guitarist then, was very bluesy, while Darryl was a romantic violinist. The shows were great, but the new songs to me were mostly not as inspiring as the *Air Cut* period. Into the bargain, Miles Copeland stopped representing Curved Air, to focus on the punk upsurge.

Mutually, Curved Air decided they had gone as far as they could by the end of 1976. Some might say that the band should have been laid to rest a couple of years earlier, but their last two albums do contain songs that are worth listening to and are ultimately justified as part of Curved Air's musical legacy of the 1970s, and indeed, beyond.

The Best Of Curved Air was reviewed in *Record Mirror & Disc* in May 1976:

Curved Air were never, in my opinion, a great musical force to be reckoned with. They started off well in a welter of publicity and with a flash looking album. The music within could have done with a similar amount of afterthought. Violinist, Darryl Way, carried the band to a great extent with his exuberant expertise and gave new life to Vivaldi. However, after that one track, things fell away a bit for the band. Sonja Kristina had a good voice, a reasonable presentation but was never really projected as much as she could have been. They could have been a much better band, but there didn't appear to be a sustained effort on someone's part. 'Back Street Luv', also included here, did very well for them but should have been a jumping-off point for greater achievements.

1977-1979

After Curved Air disbanded, all members continued a rich musical career throughout the 1970s. Francis Monkman participated in the excellent supergroup project, 801, with Phil Manzanera and Brian Eno. In 1978, Monkman found success with classical guitarist John Williams and the band Sky, playing a perfect blend of classical and rock music. Francis Monkman told *Electronics & Music Maker* in March 1983: 'Something I've always been keen to do since I was about thirteen, is to write music that took in everything I like'.

It was in Sky that his compositional abilities really came to the fore; Monkman wrote more than half the music on the first album.

In addition to Monkman and Williams, the original well-known Sky line-up featured bass player Herbie Flowers; electric guitarist Kevin Peek; and drummer Tristan Fry. Sky's self-titled debut album was released in 1979. It featured versions of Eric Satie's 'Gymnopedie No. 1', and Antonio Ruiz-Pipò's 'Danza', along with original compositions by Monkman and Flowers. Monkman's 'Cannonball' was a minor hit single. He also contributed the 20-minute composition, 'Where Opposites Meet'. The track is strongly demonstrative of the band's diverse influences.

Sky toured the UK in summer and autumn 1979. Highlights included sold-out concerts at the Royal Albert Hall and the Dominion Theatre in London. In 1980, Sky recorded and released their second album, *Sky 2*. It was a double album that built upon the success of the band's debut. The album included Monkman's side-long rock suite, 'FIFO'. The piece was inspired by computer information processing techniques: 'First In, First Out'. On *Sky 2*, Bach's *Toccata A-nd Fugue* is a distinctive track; the band make it their own. It was released as a single under the name 'Toccata', and reached number 5 in the UK, giving the band the opportunity to perform on *Top Of The Pops*. There is also a cover of Curved Air's 'Vivaldi' on *Sky 2*. Having scored success with his soundtrack for the film *The Long Good Friday*, Monkman left Sky in 1980 to focus on his own projects.

Now doing session work, Darryl Way contributed his excellent violin skills to Jethro Tull's 1978 folk-rock masterpiece, *Heavy Horses* (Way played on the tracks 'Acres Wild' and 'Heavy Horses'). Way told *Goldmine* in September 2018: 'The four-week tour in America led to a friendship with Ian Anderson. Ian is a perfectionist. We did several takes on each of the songs'.

Way's other session work around this time included playing violin on Gong's *Expresso 2* and *Time Is The Key* albums, Wayne County And The Electric Chairs' *Storm The Gates Of Heaven*, and Marianne Faithfull's *Broken English*.

It was also in 1978 that Way wrote and recorded his first wholly classical piece, *Concerto For Electric Violin*. Francis Monkman provided the keyboard orchestration and Ian Mosley the percussion. This album began a number of collaboration projects between Way and Monkman; the two worked together on each of Darryl Way's next two classical projects. The concerto was also performed, sans Francis, who had other recording commitments, on *The South Bank Show* with the Royal Philharmonic Orchestra. Way also performed the concerto live on German television with the Bavarian Radio Symphony Orchestra and in England with the Northern Sinfonia. When asked how he would describe his music, Way told *Music Street Journal* in October 2013: 'Music that hopefully has an emotional effect on the listener and lifts their spirit'.

Following his time in Curved Air, Kirby Gregory formed a band called Stretch with singer, Elmer Gantry. They went on to record and produce four albums together. In 1976, Kirby wrote the single, 'Why Did You Do It?'. It achieved international success and later featured in the movie *Lock, Stock And Two Smoking Barrels*. In 1978, he recorded and produced a solo album, *Composition*. His career then diversified further as he spent the next few years working with a wide range of artists, including Gloria Mundi, Snips, Cozy Powell, Graham Bonnet and Joan Armatrading.

After Curved Air, Jim Russell formed Stretch with Kirby Gregory, recording their first album *Elastique*. After leaving Stretch, Russell worked as a session musician on albums by The Woods Band, Matthews Southern Comfort, and The Inmates.

Eddie Jobson had met Bryan Ferry early in 1973, whilst working as a session musician on Ferry's first solo album, *These Foolish Things*. When Brian Eno left Roxy Music, Ferry remembered Jobson's work and asked him to leave Curved Air in order to join Roxy Music. Jobson played on *Country Life*, *Siren* and *Viva!* during his tenure with Roxy Music. Thereafter he was in further demand as a session musician. He toured and guested on albums by Amazing Blondel, Dana Gillespie, Bryan Ferry (again), Andy McKay, Phil Manzanera, King Crimson, Roger Glover, John Entwistle and Frank Zappa. He also released a solo single in 1976: 'Yesterday Boulevard'/'On A Still Night'.

Jobson had met bassist John Wetton while playing with Roxy Music and also met drummer Bill Bruford when overdubbing violin parts on King Crimson's *USA* album in 1975. Robert Fripp decided that the three should play together, according to rumour; recruited guitarist, Alan Holdsworth, in 1977 and called the group UK. The band recorded three albums: *UK*, *Danger Money*, and the live *Night After Night*, before disbanding.

The stellar UK line-up was such that an advert Polydor placed in the music papers said of the band members: 'All their lives, they've been rehearsing for this band and this album'.

In July 1978, *Cash Box* reviewed UK's performance that took place at El Mocambo in Toronto. Notably, strong praise was given to Jobson in particular:

The term 'supergroup' has come to be known as the musical kiss of death. When applied to an upstart collection of experienced musicians, the term has been responsible for the over-hyping (and subsequent disappointing performances) of several bands during the past decade. But UK is an exception to the rule. Each band member is a proven musician who has been directly responsible for the development of progressive music. The North American debut concert – before a packed house at Toronto's El Mocambo club – almost instantly established them as a new force with which to be reckoned. In concert, the band is as fine an aggregation of progressive exponents as one will find. Vocalist/bassist John Wetton is tougher than on disc but more appealing. Guitarist Alan Holdsworth is restrained but sharp and fluid in his solos. Drummer Bill Bruford is impeccable and as fine a technician within the ranks of drummers as exists today. But the highlight of the show is Eddie Jobson, the virtuoso violinist/keyboardist for the band. His counter-play with Holdsworth's guitar, and his skyrocketing solos, are the magical cohesive factor within the group that whips the band's music on to new limits. If indeed there is a band deserving of the supergroup label, it is this one. They are bound to revive the languishing art of progressive music and excite concert audiences for a long time to come.

In early 1977, Stewart Copeland founded The Police with lead singer and bass guitarist Sting, and guitarist Henry Padovani (who was soon replaced by Andy Summers). In a July 1977 review of an early Police gig – so early that Henry Padovani was the guitarist – the journalist writing for *Record Mirror* spoke highly of Copeland's post-Curved Air performance:

'We are not a punk band, right' – drummer Stewart Copeland was adamant before Friday night's gig at The Marquee. And yes, he is right; they are no new wave wagon band, but they are fast and furious. Fast and furious and loud. At times a fraction too loud. The people who had pogo-danced to The Lurkers, mainly stood and watched a set that was steaming along at 100-mph-plus. A three-piece, Police had some of the feeling that the big trios of the sixties – Hendrix, Cream etc. – pile-drove into their music. But now, several years later, something else is required, more social commitment, and, if possible, an extra push of speed and energy. The Police are about halfway there now and show little sign of letting up. Stewart Copeland – vacationing from Curved Air – is strictly in command, building up a storm for the bass and guitar players to work around. Guitarist Padovani, provided some meaty riffs and solo excursions, but the main centre of attention was perhaps bass player Sting, clad in just a pair of dungarees, craning his neck as he swung 'round to the microphone. Their material is distinct but undistinguished. Typical is their single 'Fallout', with an interesting point to make, but not really making it clear enough. Best of the numbers was indisputably 'Dead End Job', which succeeded to put over its message loud and clear – but then we did get it three times. Somehow, Police balls will never mean the same again.

On 18 August 1977 – just a month after the above review was printed in *Record Mirror* – the iconic Police line-up of Copeland, Sting and Summers, performed for the first time at Rebecca's club in Birmingham. From there, the late 1970s would, of course, prove to be an amazing period for The Police. Released in 1978, their debut album, *Outlandos d'Amour*, got to number 6 in the UK. It was bolstered by the strength of the singles 'Roxanne' and 'Can't Stand Losing You'. In 1979, their second album, *Reggatta de Blanc*, became the first of four consecutive number 1 studio albums for the band in both the UK and Australia. The album's first two singles – 'Message In A Bottle' and 'Walking On The Moon' – were their first UK number ones.

After Curved Air split in 1976 and after releasing six studio albums with the band, Sonja Kristina worked various jobs in order to support her young family prior to going back into music. In May 1978, she lent her talents as a guest musician to Mick Farren's album released in August: *Vampires Stole My Lunch Money*. Former Dr. Feelgood guitarist Wilko Johnson, also guested on it.

Regarding Sonja Kristina's return to live music, The *Reading Evening Post* reported in May 1978:

The first live performance of Sonja Kristina since the split of Curved Air two years ago took place at Bulmershe College last Saturday. It was a precursory gig to try out the band before an upcoming extensive tour in a few weeks time. Sonja was obviously anxious to be going back on stage once more; she spoke enthusiastically about her new band. It was chosen from contributors to a three-day jam that Sonja organised: 'I was looking for musicians with strong and interesting ideas who are versatile and willing to experiment. I expect people to hear a lot of different sounds tonight!', she said. Joining the band on stage, Sonja was rapturously welcomed and soon showed her voice to be in fine form, delivering some of her heaviest songs to date. The band were amazingly tight for their short existence (two weeks of rehearsals prior to the gig). She wore the familiar – although now slightly worn – costume of her last Curved Air tour, but she herself appears fresh and lively, radiating happiness. She quickly established an intimate rapport with the crowd, that lasted throughout the set and into both encores. The set contained three Curved Air numbers: 'Melinda', 'It Happened Today' and 'The Purple Speed Queen'. Of the new songs; 'Rollercoaster', with slick, fast, moving harmonies; 'Fade Away' – an inspiring mixture of styles with an emotive chorus; 'How Many Signs' – a catchy tune reminiscent of sophisticated punk, and 'San Tropez' – a good closing number – were the most memorable.

Another one of Sonja's early post-Curved Air performances was reviewed in *Newcastle Mayfair* in June 1978:

What is this, a rock band or a carnival parade? There's one guy in fishnet tights and a dicky-bow; another sports a white jump suit, Oriental makeup and hairdo. Yet another is archetype new wave – black costume, white face and bleached blonde hair. Two chicks; one in a long dress with waist-length slit, the other, a certain Miss Sonja Kristina in feathered garb, complete the picture. The drummer is quite normal, a reminder perhaps that it is music we have gathered to listen to. Sonja Kristina, you may remember, used to occupy the column inches now exclusively reserved for the delightful Debbie. With Curved Air, she established some kind of reputation, partly for the originality of the music but partly for hype and mammary displays. Now she has put together a new band, who are quite surprisingly rather good. They've got their share of problems; one of which – the atrocious sound balance – made it difficult to assess the music as a whole, but certainly, the individual playing was fine. I found most of the material ice-cold – not necessarily a fault – but the stage presentation detracted from it where it should have reinforced it. They should work on achieving an overall cohesiveness, which would match numbers like 'Villain' and 'Man He Colour' to the mystery of the old Curved Air songs such as 'It Happened Today'. In retrospect, I suppose that band was loaded with potential and brimming with ideas, which were only half worked out. If they're working at full stretch, then a little more time spent on the music, and a little less on the make-up, might help.

That's an interesting review in that it seems to offer a very mixed opinion of the gig, and there was perhaps so much going on that it may have been difficult for the reviewer to make a fair assessment of the music. Reasonably so, Sonja Kristina's reputation and fame earned from Curved Air followed through to her solo career. I would imagine that the iconic nature of her performances with Curved Air were such that any project she did thereafter would have certainly invited comparison.

One of the most endearing things about Sonja Kristina as an artist is perhaps her ongoing willingness to experiment in how she expresses her music on stage. Most Curved Air fans would probably consider that as being to her credit, even in instances where her eccentricity may have missed the mark a bit, such as the reviewer in this feature was possibly implying. Where the reviewer refers to Debbie, I suggest they perhaps meant Debbie Harry. The date lines up with my theory, but still, I state it without complete certainty.

The music press seemed keen to welcome Sonja's comeback. Under the headline, 'Sonja's Song Goes On', *Record Mirror* reported in June 1978:

Do you remember Curved Air? More to the point, do you remember Sonja Kristina – the lady whose voice used to send shivers down the spine of every male member of the audience. Apart from a one-off 'reunion' tour a couple of years ago, we haven't heard much from any of the band, which is a shame since they were a formidably talented collection. It is nice, then, to be able to report that Sonja has got herself together with a new band, and on the strength of this evening, they could, one day, eclipse Curved Air. Bear in mind that this was only their fifth gig, and that they were playing a half-full Camden Music Machine. The band came on without Sonja, settled into place, and launched into one of the most dynamite instrumentals I have ever heard. When you go to see them, don't let them go unless they play 'The Comforter'. By the time that one had sunk in, a large number of the audience had come down front to listen, even one of the pool tables was free, and that's quite a compliment. Then Sonja proceeded to reel them in. The songs are mostly new. There are a few of the best of the old – 'It Happened Today', 'Melinda (More Or Less)' and 'Purple Speed Queen' – but they have all been stripped down and rebuilt. They are much more direct and powerful than when Curved Air played them. Sonja now has a backing vocalist known as Cassandra. Moans? Well, the PA was dire, too loud, too trebly and badly balanced. Also, I don't think the band is quite together yet. But they dragged two encores out of a very tired Music Machine audience, and they gave me one of the best nights out I have had in a very long time.

Even though Curved Air had their heyday in the early 1970s, they were still a point of reference towards the end of the decade. It was considered in *Record Mirror* in January 1978:

When Darryl Way and Eddie Jobson used to fiddle for Curved Air and Roxy Music, they used the flashomatic style: the aristocratic pose that owed more to the eccentric concert violinist than it did to rock. The long coat tails, flowing hair, the slim hips thrust forward. Was there a clean white hankie under the chin? I can't remember.

Conclusion

Curved Air rose to fame through their live performances and progressive rock music. At the beginning of the band's tenure, the classical imprint of Terry Riley was combined with dynamic violin, adventurous synthesizers, energetic guitar and Sonja Kristina's uniquely mesmerising vocals. All these elements elevated Curved Air from the underground scene into the mainstream, and coupled with clever promotion of their debut album, they had ongoing success in the charts between the years 1970 and 1972. It could be said that in some ways, Curved Air's success was accelerated. It was reported in *Beat Instrumental* in March 1971:

> In a few short months, Curved Air have emerged from the unknown depths to become one of the most talked-about bands around. By a combination of record company promotion (ranging from ads, to that pretty patterned album) and a word-of-mouth reputation gained from their gigs, the group became a name before they had really done that much. Such a situation can be worrying for a band, but Curved Air have the confidence to carry on unaffected.

Along with High Tide and East Of Eden, Curved Air was one of the first rock bands after It's A Beautiful Day and The United States Of America to feature an electric violin: the inspiring and dramatic contribution of the excellent Darryl Way. On keyboards and guitar, Francis Monkman was a trailblazer for future electronica and ambient music. With Florian Pilkington-Miksa providing an expressive rhythmic pulse on the drums, Curved Air had a recognisable signature sound.

Although after 1972, Curved Air underwent many line-up changes and a number of significant stylistic changes, what they achieved overall was certainly noteworthy, and indeed, a source of inspiration for future generations of musicians. Sonja Kristina told *Record Collector* in April 2012:

> Siouxsie Sioux mentioned somewhere that she liked Curved Air, and so did Phil Oakey from The Human League. Rat Scabies wanted The Damned to cover 'Back Street Luv'. Stewart and I knew all these people from when we used to go down to The Roxy week after week. It was as exciting in its way as when I used to go to the folk clubs when I was thirteen or to Middle Earth and The Roundhouse in 1967.

Gimmicky or not, the use of the new picture disc technology to promote Curved Air's debut album, was certainly memorable. In November 1978, the *Middlesex County Times* featured an article about picture discs when – even eight years after the release of *Air Conditioning* – the visual singularity of the album had not been forgotten:

> The picture disc is the latest ploy of the record companies to try and get you to part with your money. Apparently convinced that people sit and watch records go 'round when the television becomes too tedious, they've decided to brighten up our lives by putting pictures onto them. It's now about eight years since we first saw a picture disc, in the guise of the first Curved Air album. But as you'll remember, if you possess that collector's item, the record was very heavy, and the sound quality was none too clever ... The method needed a complex five-layer sandwich of paper and vinyl to get the right visual effect, which made the process very time-consuming and not so commercially viable.

The article went on to describe how Warner Bros. were using new technology to make picture discs; in this instance, a new 1978 single by The Cars (with, fittingly, a picture of a car on it!). Besides, in the music newspapers at the time of the *Air Conditioning* picture disc, the advert stated: 'A great new revolutionary group, Curved Air, deserve a great new revolutionary record'.

As was reported in *Cash Box* in August 1978:

> With the impending release of the film, *Sgt. Pepper's Lonely Hearts Club Band*, set for October here, EMI is gearing to generate new sales of the classic Beatles albums with a limited release of a picture disc. This will be the first UK picture disc since Warner Brothers released the debut album from Curved Air eight years ago.

Whilst the picture disc technology may have been rarely used due to the technology being primitive and the overheads involved, if such a marketing approach was good enough for The Beatles, it was certainly good enough for Curved Air (or vice versa, depending on how you look at it).

'Back Street Luv' was a tremendous shot in the arm for Curved Air's career. It is the song they are probably best remembered for. In *Prog* in March 2015, Sonja Kristina described people's reaction to the song:

It was amazing. When it was released, I recall hearing it on Alan Freeman's Saturday afternoon show on Radio One, and I had a feeling then it would catch on. It got a lot of radio airplay after that and people really took to the song. It was a blessing. The song seems to reach out to our fans even now. Every time we play it, 'Back Street Luv' gets a massive reaction. Like every hit single, this obviously means something different to each person. I know where it comes from, of course, however, the fact it has resonated down the years is a big compliment. It's a simple song, but then those are often the ones to stand the test of time. I had been to a Beatles gig at a theatre in Wembley when they got loads of screaming girls. But what we got were screaming boys. We were used to having audiences who would listen to our songs and then applaud. But now, they would go crazy for us. We even got to do *Top Of The Pops*. It was all new territory for Curved Air.

It comes across that Curved Air – even during the height of their success – always had a somewhat difficult relationship with their critics and the record-buying public. Sonja Kristina told *Beat Instrumental* in June 1972:

You know that the prejudice is there, but you can't afford to let it bring you down. You can't let it put you off. You realise that there are people who want to see you. You have to ignore the criticism, go out there on stage and do your best. In this business, you can't afford to compromise.

In the same feature, Sonja touched on the idea that despite some of the derogatory labels attached to Curved Air and their music (for instance; gimmicky, hyped, middle-class rock, pomp rock), there wasn't a specific remit set out within the band in regard to wanting to make a particular statement or sound:

I really have no idea what Curved Air are about. Not at least, in definite terms. The musical thing stems from Darryl and Francis. They do most of the writing. Although Mike Wedgwood, who joined us as bassist early this year, is also writing some material. I don't think the music sets out to establish anything. It just represents the way things are at the time. Above that, we simply set out to play whatever is interesting, enjoyable and appropriate.

In *Beat Instrumental* in March 1971, Darryl Way addressed the interviewer's comment that some may see Curved Air's music as a fusion of pop and classical:

> I don't like to think of it like that. We're just using what we've learnt, and there are a variety of influences in the band. Francis and I have gone through a lot of musical stages through being taught classical music. Sonja was in folk and singing in *Hair*. Ian's a rock bass player. The classical thing isn't conscious at all. I don't want to try and fuse the two; it's pointless. Barriers are breaking down anyway. Everyone gets tagged, I suppose, but audiences take in what they hear. They like it, or they don't. They don't apply tags; it's only critics and pop papers that do that!

Although Curved Air's music is most often filed under the category of progressive rock, by today's standards and use of the term, I think it is important to be mindful of the fact that, essentially, the band themselves were perhaps not necessarily aiming for a particular labelling of their music, or to fit within a certain musical brand or genre. It seems that if they liked it and they had the skills to put it across – both on record and live – they did it.

Even if you subscribe to the notion that Curved Air were hyped – at least due to how their debut album was promoted – there was certainly an extent to which they had to live up to such hype musically. With talent and self-assurance, they managed to do just that, at least during the early 1970s. Darryl Way told *Beat Instrumental* in March 1971:

> It's a new game for all of us, except for Ian Eyre and Sonja. We've enough confidence in our music, and the hype hasn't worried us. We've always felt we could match the expectations. Whatever the goal that's been put in front of us, we've set out to achieve it. It's been a strain, but we've not been worried that we couldn't fulfil the promises.

As a result of some critics saying the band's first album was hyped and that their music was pretentious due to the classical influences present, Darryl Way addressed the issue:

> A lot of things have been printed that sound pretentious when quoted but which weren't in the context they were said. It's very difficult. When you're getting misquoted and sensationalised, you tend to end up saying

'yes' or 'no', just clamming up. I'm getting very wary of interviews since things have been put down wrongly. The last thing we want to be is pretentious or intellectual about the group.

Unable to sustain life in the premier league of progressive rock after one seminal but solitary top five single – 'Back Street Luv' – and three initial top 20 albums, the ever-evolving Curved Air remained as the stomping ground for sultry singer, Sonja Kristina, and a host of other talented musicians.

The founding band members proceeded to work together on a number of each others' solo projects during the 1980s. Darryl Way appeared on Sonja Kristina's first solo album in 1980 and on Francis Monkman's *Dweller On The Threshold* in 1981. In 1983, Way returned to rock, writing a number of new songs. He recorded a 3-song EP of somewhat dance-oriented, synthesized tracks called 'As Long As There's A Spark', featuring himself on lead vocals. This was followed by the single, 'Little Plum', which was in the same musical vein. It was, and is, a very catchy instrumental, which, with a bit more airplay, could plausibly have seen chart success. Two of the songs Darryl wrote during this period were 'Renegade' and 'We're Only Human', which he felt needed a female vocal. He asked Sonja to record them with him, and they decided to resurrect the Curved Air name for the single. Darryl and Sonja worked on one more piece together in the 1980s: 'O Fortuna'. It was written by classical composer Carl Orff, as part of his masterwork, *Carmina Burana*. Darryl Way's arrangement was released as the B-side of Sonja Kristina's 'Walk On By' 12" single. Oddly, executors of the Orff estate sued to have distribution of the single stopped.

Returning to classical forms, Darryl Way again joined forces with Francis Monkman to produce *The Human Condition* in 1987. Written and conducted by Way, the piece is an emotional eight-part suite featuring Way on violin, Monkman on piano and classical ensemble, Opus 20. Way did more sessions following the release of *The Human Condition*, including producing *Music Without Frontiers* and playing violin on Boris Grebenshikov's *Radio Silence*.

After his time with UK, Eddie Jobson continued with sessions and contributed keyboards, electric violin and synthesizer to Jethro Tull's 1980 album, *A*. Jobson told *Keyboard* in November 2016:

As for playing with Jethro Tull, they were such a good group of British gentlemen – solid musicians and super-professional on tour. Ian

Anderson and I became friends after UK toured with them, enough that he invited me to collaborate with him on his first solo album. Of course, as it wasn't a Tull album.

It was after his time working with Jethro Tull that Jobson started his own band, Zinc. They recorded one album: *The Green Album*, released in 1983. After Zinc, Jobson began working with new age music. He recorded his second solo LP – *Theme Of Secrets* – in such a guise. Later in his long-standing career, Jobson wrote music for television. This included an ongoing role as musical director of the American TV series *Nash Bridges*.

After playing in Kiki Dee's backing band on Elton John's *Goodbye Yellow Brick Road* tour in the UK – and recording Elton's song, 'Hard Luck Story' with Dee's band – Mike Wedgwood joined Caravan in 1974. He remained with them until 1976, playing on the albums *Live At Fairfield Halls* (recorded in 1974 and released by Decca in 2002, it was actually his debut with Caravan), *Cunning Stunts* and *Blind Dog At St Dunstans*.

Whilst The Police were one of the top bands of the 1980s, more recently, Stewart Copeland has produced film soundtracks, as well as the soundtracks for the *Spyro* video game series. He has also written various pieces of music for ballet, opera and orchestra. When Curved Air lost Copeland to The Police, it ultimately left the Curved Air name in limbo until 1984, when Darryl Way invited Sonja Kristina to sing on his new venture, the 'Renegade' single (with 'We're Only Human' on the B-side). Copeland and Kristina divorced in 1991 after seven years of marriage. Copeland told *Cash Box* in November 1980:

> My experience in Curved Air helped us avoid a lot of the mistakes a young band can make. Specifically, selling yourself for dollars up-front before you've got a musical identity. Many groups are so eager to get the advance that they don't check out royalty rates, and they end up selling themselves.

It seems that during his time with Curved Air, Stewart Copeland learned what not to do when it came to being a founding member of The Police. That said, it could be that without Copeland having been in Curved Air, The Police might not have come to be. Curved Air was, after all, the beginning of a long and successful career for Copeland.

Although Sonja Kristina's Escape were active as a live band in 1978, it wasn't until 1980 that an album was released. Sonja told *Record Collector* in April 2012:

I got Sonja Kristina's Escape together, which was financed by Roy Thomas Baker, Queen's producer, who was keen to produce my first solo album. He presented some finished tracks to CBS, but they didn't take it up. So I recorded the album with Nigel Gray, who produced The Police. It was titled *Sonja Kristina*, but it was me and the musicians from Escape, which was very different from Curved Air. Recently, my son said it reminded him of Talking Heads.

Freddie Mercury was also a big help to Sonja Kristina in getting her first solo album off the ground in 1980. Sonja told *Hit Channel* in December 2018:

I met Freddie Mercury because I wanted to record my own solo album after Curved Air had broken up. So, I asked Roy Thomas Baker, who produced Queen – I ran into him at a social gathering and I think Freddie was there too – if he would produce an album with me, and he said he would. He asked me to work on some tracks together, three tracks, and he took them to the record company he was working with then, but they didn't fit them up and he left to do a different project, but he financed my band, Escape, to go on tour, so that was a good thing. I learned a lot about how Freddie worked, that he was very much a perfectionist, so that he prepared things for quite long before he goes in the studio and he was ready to record. I think Freddie had a fantastic voice. He's one of my heroes. He was a fantastic performer. Extravaganza and big energy.

It wasn't until 1980 and the release of her self-titled solo album, that Sonja Kristina was able to show a wider audience that she had lost none of her talent.
Ever the creative outside of Curved Air, Sonja has done a whole range of projects. She told *Record Collector* in April 2012:

After Escape, I fronted Tunis: a young prog-rock outfit local to where Stewart and I were living near High Wycombe. Our set consisted of some new songs I'd written and Curved Air stuff. There were also two one-shot singles: 'Renegade', credited to Curved Air, but actually just me with Darryl playing all the instruments; and 'Walk On By', produced by William Orbit, who became most renowned for his work with Madonna. In between times, I was Juliet in *Romeo And Juliet* and toured with Helen Shapiro and Amanda Barrie in *The French Have A Song For It*: a musical of translated chansons by Jacques Brel, Georges Brassens and Edith Piaf, among others. That ended up in the West End. I also starred in a musical by Marsha Hunt called *Man To Woman*. Also a musical drama for TV called *Curiculee Curicula*. In 1988, I played a schizophrenic in an award-winning play, *Shona*, at the Pentameter in Hampstead. That was when I was getting the acid-folk band together. My youngest child was old enough for me to go out looking for an outlet for writing and performing again. I went back to The Troubadour, where they were launching an album by the best of the regular performers there, called *In The Beginning Tommy Steele*. None were household names, but they had everything – interesting songs, charisma – and I wanted to be part of it. I started working with some of them, but I needed more than just the acoustic energy. It was then that I also discovered the psychedelic venues such as The Crypt in Deptford, and Club Dog in Finsbury Park, with the light shows and multimedia acts, rather like Middle Earth and The UFO in the 60s. Ozric Tentacles were the most popular headliners there. Under a pseudonym – Nodens Ictus – they supported when the old Curved Air reunited once more in 1990. We were approached to appear on a TV series about classic rock bands, but it didn't materialise. An in-concert album came out of it, albeit recorded directly off the mixing desk, with Francis doing what he could with it afterwards. Yet, I was glad we were able to immortalise that moment.

Sonja credited Curved Air accordingly for the career opportunities it presented her with outside the band. She told the *Harrogate Advertiser* in September 2018:

The main buzz for me was always performing. I'm quite a private person. I'd hang out with my own crowd. The band didn't get pursued by the press like later on when my ex-husband Stewart Copeland was in The Police. We did get invited to record industry parties. I remember being at a Warner Brothers one, and there was Joni Mitchell, which was quite exciting. I didn't go across and talk to her though … Over the years, I've been spoiled by the standard of musicianship. I feel, in my life, I was very lucky to be in the musical Hair, then lucky to meet Darryl and Francis and the band, and then to get invited to be their singer. They were such gifted boys.

Sonja Kristina's candour about the music industry and how she relates to it often comes across in an endearing way in interviews. She told *Prog* in February 2018:

> On stage, I do get a rush, which gives me extra confidence. I am nervous before a performance. But once it starts, I am in the zone and focused. But when I am offstage, I am not particularly sociable. I tend not to be good at parties when I don't know anyone – unless I have consumed substances! But I am fine in one-to-one situations.

In the same interview, Sonja explained how she psyched herself up prior to going on stage:

> This might sound odd, but I had a skipping rope that I'd use before going onstage. I would use it to get my energy levels right up, and that was a great way of preparing. Simple but effective.

With all of her performing experience, teaching was a natural progression. Sonja Kristina taught performing arts at Middlesex University during the 1990s. She told *Prog* in February 2018:

> Oh, I loved it. Because what I was doing was teaching on a one-to-one level. If you put me in front of a class and asked me to teach, then I would be totally lost. If you have a big group, then they'd all be at different levels, and inevitably some of the students would be disruptive, and they would all have differing tastes. That was never for me, which is why I could not work in that situation with a choir. But I am a natural when dealing with one pupil at a time, as happened at Middlesex University. I had my own music room and it was bliss. I even got to find out a lot about jazz from being there, a type of music I knew little about beforehand. I still teach, although not there.

As was reported in *Record Collector* in April 2012:

> Sonja's professional activities have also included studying for an MA in performing arts, and teaming up with modern classical composer, producer and multi-instrumentalist, Marvin Ayres, as MASK, for 2005's *Heavy Petal* and 2010's *Technopia*. While embracing the experimental essence of Curved Air, those albums are further from 'Back Street Luv'

than could be imagined by those attendant at the band's standing-room-only engagements – shows that are as much celebrations of Sonja's career as they are the group.

All areas of the performing arts have been a large part of Sonja Kristina's career. She told *Prog* in February 2018:

> I did learn a certain amount at drama school. But in *Hair*, we learned to use our energy to fill the space, to trust one another, while relating truthfully as people. We were also encouraged to be spontaneous and to leave everything of ourselves on that stage. I was into singing at the drop of a hat. Even when I was in *Hair*, I'd go along to restaurants with friends and would take little encouraging to strum a few songs. I never thought musical theatre was for me. I did a couple of other theatrical productions like *The French Have A Song For It* (1979) and *Man To Woman* (1982), but that was never where I saw myself going full time.

Curved Air regrouped in 1990 and released a live recording, *Alive*. It featured the line-up of Sonja Kristina, Francis Monkman, Florian Pilkington-Miksa, Darryl Way and Rob Martin. It was recorded at a one-off gig at London's Town & Country. In 2008, they once again made plans to reunite for a number of summer UK gigs and festivals. The plan went ahead, but Francis Monkman (himself superseded by the younger Andy Christie on guitar and Chris Harris on bass) revamped some of the band's better-known numbers for comeback studio set, *Reborn*. Still going strong and with a newfound energy and vitality, *Live Atmosphere* was released in 2012, with Kit Morgan on guitar.

The long-awaited studio set, *North Star*, was released in 2014 and was, to many Curved Air fans, a welcome addition to their collection. Down to just Sonja, Florian, and fellow writers Chris Harris, Paul Sax and Robert Norton (Kirby Gregory played in session), the album proved that the band still had something to offer as a group of talented musicians doing what they do best. The tracks, 'Stay Human', 'Images And Signs' and 'Spiders', have all the hallmarks of the original Curved Air sound, whilst the inclusion of covers: The Police' 'Spirits In The Material World', Snow Patrol's 'Chasing Cars' and The Beatles' 'Across The Universe', offer something different. At the time of writing this book (winter 2019), Curved Air exist in the form of a live touring band. The present line-up consists of Sonja Kristina, Chris Harris (bass), Robert Norton (keyboards), Andy Tween (drums), Grzegorz Gadziomski (violin) and Kirby Gregory (guitar).

Curved Air is perhaps generally viewed as a forgotten footnote in progressive rock. From the beginning of their tenure in the 1970s, there was certainly very mixed feelings towards the band from both the music-buying public and the media. Some considered that Curved Air were a hyped band who were overdoing it with the classical thing, whilst others saw the band as a breath of fresh air; a team of talented musicians offering an interesting sound with much creativity and innovation. Members in the later line-ups, Eddie Jobson and Stewart Copeland went on to achieve great fame elsewhere. It is plausible that their successes as individuals perhaps overshadow Curved Air's legacy. Overall though, the core nucleus of Francis Monkman, Darryl Way, Florian Pilkington-Miksa and Sonja Kristina put out a trio of exciting albums that were notable for a number of great songs and some daring attempts at classical and rock fusion. Whether based on a deliberate musical remit or simply as being the result of their tastes and preferences, Curved Air put out some fantastic music that is well worth a listen. It was then, and it is now. Equally, where chart success is not the be-all-and-end-all, and where all of Curved Air's line-ups included talent and innovation, all of their discography is certainly with merit.

They created a compelling mixture of hard rock and classical music that predominantly saw them labelled as a progressive rock band. There were times in the band's tenure when, commercially, their image and sound went in their favour and times when their work didn't quite hit the mark on a broader scale. Line-up changes made the band, for many, perhaps seem like Sonja Kristina with a backing band, but essentially – household names or not – there was a tremendous amount of talent in Curved Air, and every line-up recorded fascinating and worthwhile albums. Curved Air's 1970's tenure was arguably their most prolific, hence the scope of this book. Still, their legacy will live on; both in terms of projects that all band members did outside of the band, and indeed, in terms of what Curved Air contributed to music during the 1970s and thereafter.

Appendices

Curved Air Singles

'It Happened Today'/'Vivaldi'/'What Happens When You Blow Yourself Up' (Warner Bros. WB 8023) 1971

'Back Street Luv'/'Everdance' (Warner Bros. WB 8029) 1971

'Sarah's Concern'/'Phantasmagoria' (Warner Bros. K 16164) 1972

'Back Street Luv'/'It Happened Today'/'Marie Antoinette'/'Ultra Vivaldi' (Warner Bros. K 16412) 1974

'Back Street Luv'/'Everdance' (Warner Bros. K 16092) 1974

'Back Street Luv'/'It Happened Today (live)' (Deram DM 426) 1975

'Desiree'/'Kids To Blame' (BTM SBT 103) 1976

'Baby Please Don't Go'/'Broken Lady' (BTM SBT 106) 1976

Line-ups
January-April 1970
Sonja Kristina: vocals
Rob Martin: bass guitar
Francis Monkman: keyboards, guitar
Florian Pilkington Miksa: drums
Darryl Way: violin, keyboards, backing vocals

April 1970-Late 1971
Sonja Kristina: vocals
Francis Monkman: keyboards, guitar
Florian Pilkington-Miksa: drums
Darryl Way: violin, keyboards, backing vocals
Ian Eyre: bass guitar
Additional personnel:
Barry de Souza: drums (filled in for Pilkington-Miksa – 1971)

Late 1971-Late 1972
Sonja Kristina: vocals
Francis Monkman: keyboards, guitar
Florian Pilkington-Miksa: drums
Darryl Way: violin, keyboards, backing vocals
Mike Wedgwood: bass guitar, vocals, guitar

Late 1972-Summer 1973
Sonja Kristina: vocals, acoustic guitar
Mike Wedgwood: bass guitar, vocals, guitar
Eddie Jobson: keyboards, violin
Kirby Gregory: guitar
Jim Russell: drums

Summer 1973
Sonja Kristina: vocals, acoustic guitar
Mike Wedgwood: bass guitar, vocals, guitar
Eddie Jobson: keyboards, violin

Summer 1973-September 1974
Disbanded

September 1974-December 1974
Sonja Kristina: vocals
Phil Kohn: bass guitar
Francis Monkman: keyboards, guitar
Florian Pilkington-Miksa: drums
Darryl Way: violin, keyboards, backing vocals

Late 1974-Early 1975
Sonja Kristina: vocals
Phil Kohn: bass guitar
Darryl Way: violin, keyboards, backing vocals
Stewart Copeland: drums
Mick Jacques: guitars

Early 1975-Late 1975
Sonja Kristina: vocals
Darryl Way: violin, keyboards, backing vocals
Stewart Copeland: drums
Mick Jacques: guitars

Late 1975-Late 1976
Sonja Kristina: vocals
Darryl Way: violin, keyboards, backing vocals
Stewart Copeland: drums
Mick Jacques: guitars
Tony Reeves: bass

Late 1976
Sonja Kristina: vocals
Stewart Copeland: drums
Mick Jacques: guitars
Tony Reeves: bass
Alex Richman: keyboards

1976-1984
Disbanded

Tour Dates
1970
12-Jul: Mini Friar Café and then Cloud 9 Club Bridge Street, Peterborough
06-Sep: London Roundhouse. With Tyrannosaurus Rex, Steamhammer & others
12-Sep: Temple Club, London
15-Sep: London Roundhouse. With Heads Hands & Feet, Quiver, Mott The Hoople
23-Sep: London Northern Polytechnic. With Mott The Hoople, IF, Hawkwind and Principal Edwards
06-Nov: Salford University, Manchester with Genesis
20-Nov: Fairfield Hall, Croydon
22-Nov: Mott The Hoople Implosion, London Roundhouse. With Stoneground, Quiver Shawn Philips, Jeff Dexter
26-Nov: Mayfair Ballroom, Newcastle. Supporting The Who
30-Nov: Civic Hall, Dunstable
01-Dec: The Fickle Pickle Club, Alexandra Hotel, Southend
12-Dec: Carshalton College of Further Education Students Union. Support band – Quiver
16-Dec: High Wycombe Grammar School
19-Dec: Potters Bar Farx
28-Dec: Edmonton Cooks Ferry Inn, Edmonton

1971
03-Jan: Fox at Greyhound, Croydon, London. Supporting Yes
05-Jan: Royal Albert Hall, London. Supporting Black Sabbath and Freedom (Cancelled)
07-Jan: City Hall, Hull (Curved Air were scheduled but didn't appear). Supporting Black Sabbath and Freedom
08-Jan: Town Hall, Birmingham. Supporting Black Sabbath and Freedom
09-Jan: Colston Hall, Bristol. Supporting Black Sabbath and Freedom
11-Jan: Guildhall, Southampton. Supporting Black Sabbath and Freedom
14-Jan: Sheffield City Hall. Supporting Black Sabbath and Freedom
15-Jan: Empire Theatre, Edinburgh. Supporting Black Sabbath and Freedom
16-Jan: Music Hall, Aberdeen. Supporting Black Sabbath and Freedom
18-Jan: City Hall, Newcastle. Supporting Black Sabbath and Freedom
19-Jan: Albert Hall, Nottingham. Supporting Black Sabbath and Freedom

20-Jan: Free Trade Hall, Manchester. Supporting Black Sabbath and Freedom

23-Jan: Leeds University. Supporting Black Sabbath and Freedom

30-Jan: Fillmore East, USA. Supporting ELP and Edgar Winter's White Trash

01-Feb: Southampton University

06-Feb: Manchester Institute of Science and Technology

08-Feb: Dunstable Civic Hall

09-Feb: Crawley Starlight, Sussex

10-Feb: Tunbridge Wells Civic Hall

12-Feb: Bath University

13-Feb: Bradford University

17-Feb: Potters Bar Farx

19-Feb: Devizes Town Hall

20-Feb: Manchester University-Cochise

26-Feb: York University

27-Feb: Nelson Imperial Hall, Lancashire

03-Apr: Kiel Convention Center, St Louis, USA. Supporting Jethro Tull and Procul Harum

09-Apr: Cleveland Arena, Ohio, USA. Supporting Jethro Tull (Cactus was also on the bill)

10-Apr: Cincinnati Gardens, Ohio, USA. Supporting Jethro Tull

14-Apr: Uihlein Hall, Milwaukee, USA. Supporting Jethro Tull (two shows)

16-Apr: Pirates World Park, Fort Lauderdale, Florida, USA. Supporting Jethro Tull

17-Apr: Pirates World Park, Fort Lauderdale Florida, USA. Supporting Jethro Tull

18-Apr: Civic Centre, Roanake Virginia, USA. Supporting Jethro Tull

20-Apr: State Fairground Coliseum, Detroit, Michigan, USA. Supporting Jethro Tull

23-Apr: Eastown Theatre, Detroit, USA. With ELP, Crowbar and Sweat Hog

24-Apr: Eastown Theatre, Detroit, USA. With ELP, Crowbar and Sweat Hog

25-Apr: State University of New York, Stony Brook, USA. Supporting Jethro Tull

26-Apr: C W Post College Dome, Greenvale, NY, USA. Supporting Jethro Tull

27-Apr: Capital Theatre, Port Chester, New York, USA. Supporting Jethro Tull (two shows)

01-May: Fillmore East, New York. Supporting Jethro Tull, ELP and Edgar Winter's White Trash

07-May: The Warehouse, New Orleans. Supporting Johnny Winter and BB King

18-May: Edmonton Sundown, London

18-May: Mayfair Ballroom, Newcastle. Supporting The Who

24-May: The Guildhall, Portsmouth

03-June: Olympia Paris, France

04-June: City Hall, Hull

10-June: Town Hall, Oxford

12-June: Town Hall, Leeds

14-June: Colston Hall, Bristol

15-June: Philharmonic Hall, Liverpool

16-June: City Hall, Sheffield

18-June: Mayfair, Newcastle

19-June: St Andrew Hall, Norwich

20-June: Free Trade Hall, Manchester

21-June: Guildhall, Southampton

23-June: Town Hall, Birmingham

24-June: Guildhall, Portsmouth

25-June: Royal Festival Hall, London

28-June: Civic Hall, Dunstable

29-June: De Montfort Hall, Leicester

30-June: Civic Hall, Guildford

03-July: Winter Gardens, Weston

01-Aug: Town Hall, Birmingham. Supporting Black Sabbath and Freedom

04-Aug: Mayfair Ballroom, Newcastle. Support act, Medicine Head

27-Aug: The Weeley Festival, Clacton-on-Sea, Essex

03-Oct: Kinema, Dunfermline, Scotland

09-Oct: Leeds University. Support band America

19-Oct: Civic Centre, Springfield, Massachusetts, USA. Supporting Jethro Tull

05-Nov: William and Mary College Fieldhouse, Williamsburg, USA. Supporting Jethro Tull

06-Nov: Carmichael Auditorium, University of North Carolina, Chapel Hill, USA. Supporting Jethro Tull

07-Nov: Minges Coliseum, East Carolina, Greenville, USA. Supporting Jethro Tull

08-Nov: Coliseum, Greensboro, USA. Supporting Jethro Tull

09-Nov: Robertson Memorial Fieldhouse, Bradley, Peonia, USA. Supporting Jethro Tull

10-Nov: IMA Sports Arena, Flint, Michigan, USA. Supporting Jethro Tull

11-Nov: Mid-South Coliseum, Memphis, Tennessee, USA, Supporting Jethro Tull

12-Nov: Convention Center, Louisville, Kentucky, USA. Supporting Jethro Tull

13-Nov: Public Hall, Cleveland, Ohio, USA. Supporting Jethro Tull

14-Nov: Civic Centre, Baltimore, USA. Supporting Jethro Tull

15-Nov: Boston Garden, Massachusetts, USA. Supporting Jethro Tull

19-Nov: Hirsch Memorial Coliseum, Shreveport, Louisiana, USA. Supporting ELP

21-Nov: Cobo Arena, Detroit, Michigan, USA. Supporting Ten Years After and J Geil's Band

22-Nov: The Rainbow Theatre, London

19-Dec: City Hall, Newcastle

20-Dec: The Dome, Brighton

1972

29-Jan: Starlight Rooms, Boston, UK. Supporting Yes

04-Feb: Lyceum, London. With East of Eden, Stackridge and Audience

05-Feb: Lyceum, London. With East of Eden, Stackridge and Audience

28-Mar: The Dome, Brighton. Support from Gary Moore Band

29-Mar: Birmingham Town Hall. Support from Gary Moore Band

15-Apr: Empire Theatre, Edinburgh. Supporting Black Sabbath and Freedom

18-Apr: City Hall, Newcastle

07-May: Alexandra Palace, London

03-Jun: Corn Exchange, Cambridge

08-Jul: Center Arena, Seattle, Washington, USA. With Deep Purple and Malo

11-Jul: Palace Theatre Providence, Rhode Island, USA. With Deep Purple and John Kay

18-Jul: Bayfront Center Arena, St Petersburg, Florida. With Deep Purple and John Kay

22-Jul: Ungano's Ritz Theatre, Staten Island, New York. With Buddy Miles Express

11-13 Aug: Reading Festival (Headlining)

22-Aug: Capital Theatre Passaic, New Jersey USA. With Deep Purple & Elf

27-Aug: Rainbow Pavillion, Torquay

03-Sep: Chelsea Village Concert Hall, Bournemouth. Genesis as support

16-Sep: Buxton Pop Festival, Booth Farm. (Curved Air cancelled)
07-Oct: South Parade Theatre, Southsea
11-Oct: Liverpool Stadium. With Greasy Bear and possibly Smith, Perkins and Smith
27-Oct: Hatfield Polytechnic, Hertford

1973
01-Apr: Birmingham Town Hall
02-Apr: Sheffield City Hall
06-Apr: Hastings Pier
12-Apr: Liverpool Stadium. Support band for Nick Pickett
15-May: National Stadium, Dublin
10-May: Essex University, Colchester
11-May: Mayfair Ballroom, Newcastle. Support band was Gary Moore
21-Jul: Summer Rock Festival, Frankfurt, Germany. (two day festival)
30-Dec: Hastings Pier

1974
08-Nov: Maidstone College of Art
09-Nov: Loughborough University
10-Nov: Nottingham University
12-Nov: Top Of The World, Stafford
15-Nov: Aston University, Birmingham
20-Nov: Surrey University, Guildford
21-Nov: Polytechnic of Central London
22-Nov: Mayfair Ballroom, Newcastle. Billed as The Original Curved Air
23-Nov: Bradford University
24-Nov: Liverpool Stadium
27-Nov: Manchester University
29-Nov: Queen Mary's College London
30-Nov: Pier Pavilion, Hastings
03-Dec: Locarno, Portsmouth
04-Dec: Cardiff University
05-Dec: Bristol Polytechnic
06-Dec: Polytechnic Union, Coventry
07-Dec: Leas Cliff Town Hall, Folkestone

1975
15-Jan: Paard van Troje Den Haag, The Netherlands

16-Jan: Cultureel Centrum Amstelveen, The Netherlands
17-Jan: De Lindenberg Nijmegen, The Netherlands
18-Jan: Paradiso Amsterdam, The Netherlands
19-Jan: Swalmerstraat Roermond, The Netherlands
20-Feb: Town Hall, Watford
21-Feb: City Hall, Newcastle
22-Feb: Strathclyde University, Glasgow
24-Feb: Free Trade Hall, Manchester
25-Feb: Reading University
26-Feb: Civic Hall, Guildford
28-Feb: Southbank Polytechnic, London
01-Mar: Leeds University
03-Mar: Town Hall, Birmingham
04-Mar: Town Hall, Hove
07-Mar: Brunel University, Uxbridge
08-Mar: Corn Exchange, Cambridge
09-Mar: Central Hall, Chatham
10-Mar: Hull University
13-Mar: Leicester University
14-Mar: Sheffield University
15-Mar: St Andrews Hall, Norwich
16-Mar: Gaumont, Ipswich
17-Mar: Branwin Hall, Swansea
18-Mar: Top Rank, Cardiff
19-Mar: Liverpool University
20-Mar: Bristol University
21-Mar: Guildhall, Plymouth
22-Mar: Torquay Town Hall
24-Mar: Johnson Hall, Yeovil
25-Mar: Heavy Steam Machine, Stoke-on-Trent
27-Mar: Winter Gardens, Malvern
29-Mar: City Hall, St Albans
30-Mar: Greyhound, Croydon
10-Jun: Cambridge University
13-Jun: The Mayfair Ballroom, Newcastle
19-Jun: Locarno, Portsmouth
20-Jun: Royal Holloway College, Egham
21-Jun: Oxford University
25-Jun: Town Hall, Birmingham

27-Jun: Top Rank, Southampton
28-Jun: Kursaal, Southend-on-Sea
29-Jun: Greyhound, Croydon
26-Jul: Paradiso, Amsterdam
31-Aug: Palace Lido, Douglas
20-Sep: Pier Pavilion, Hastings
26-Sep: City Hall, St Albans
02-Oct: Bristol Polytechnic
03-Oct: Aston University, Birmingham
04-Oct: Durham University
08-Oct: Surrey University, Guildford
10-Oct: Surrey University, Guildford
18-Oct: Loughborough University
19-Oct: Roundhouse, London
23-Oct: Warwick University, Coventry
24-Oct: Brunel University, Uxbridge
25-Oct: Kursaal, Southend-on-Sea
31-Oct: Thames Polytechnic, London
08-Nov: Durham University
14-Nov: Aberystwyth University
30-Nov: Croydon Greyhound
04-Dec: Reading University
05-Dec: Salford University
06-Dec: Lancaster University
09-Dec: Town Hall, Birmingham
10-Dec: Keele University, Stoke-on-Trent
11-Dec: Brighton Dome
12-Dec: Thames Polytechnic, London
13-Dec: Leascliffe Town Hall, Folkestone
15-Dec: Colston Hall, Bristol
19-Dec: Town Hall, Leeds
21-Dec: Civic Centre, Wolverhampton
26-Dec: Holstenhalle, Neumünster
27-Dec: Niedersachsenhalle, Hannover
28-Dec: Rhein-Neckar-Halle, Heidelberg

1976

09-Jan: Nelson's Column, London
10-Jan: University of Nottingham

11-Jan: Hemel Hempstead
15-Jan: North Staffs Polytechnic, Stoke-on-Trent
17-Jan: Leicester Polytechnic
21-Jan: Kings Hall, Derby
23-Jan: Corn Exchange, Cambridge
24-Jan: Southampton University
29-Jan: Paris Theatre, London
30-Jan: Bath University
31-Jan: Sheffield University
01-Feb: Croydon Greyhound
30-Apr: Sporthal de Meenthe Steenwijk, The Netherlands
01-May: Nordmarkhalle, Rendsburg, Germany
02-May: Münsterlandhalle, Cloppenburg, Germany
04-May: Redoutensaal, Erlangen, Germany
06-May: Gustav-Siegle-Haus, Stuttgart, Germany
07-May: Rosengarten, Mannheim, Germany
08-May: Niedersachsenhalle, Hannover, Germany
09-May: Quartier Latin, Berlin, Germany
28-May: Assembly Hall Theatre, Tunbridge Wells
29-May: Skindles, Maidenhead
30-May: Roundhouse, London
31-May: Roundhouse, London
05-Jun: University of East Anglia, Norwich
06-Jun: Civic Hall, Guildford
10-Jun: Drill Hall, Lincoln
11-Jun: The Mayfair Ballroom, Newcastle
15-Jun: Bath Pavilion
16-Jun: Johnson Hall, Yeovil
17-Jun: Town Hall, Torquay
18-Jun: Pier Pavilion, Hastings
19-Jun: Kursaal, Southend-on-Sea
20-Jun: Fairfield Halls, Croydon
23-Jun: Civic Hall, Dunstable
24-Jun: Winter Gardens, Cleethorpes
25-Jun: Hull University
27-Jun: Coatham Bowl, Redcar
01-Jul: De Montfort Hall, Leicester
02-Jul: West Runton Pavilion
03-Jul: Leascliffe Town Hall, Folkestone

10-Jul: Müngersdorfer Stadion, Cologne, Germany
14-Aug: Wilhelmshaven, Germany
28-Aug: Baarlo, Holland
29-Aug: Schagen, Holland
31-Aug: Deutschlandhalle, Berlin, Germany
03-Sep: Paradiso, Amsterdam, Holland
11-Sep: Openluchttheater, Lochem, Holland
18-Sep: Oasis Club, Ryde , Isle of Wight
24-Sep: Newcastle Polytechnic
26-Sep: Ilkley
01-Oct: Top Rank, Cardiff
02-Oct: Manchester University
08-Oct: Bradford University
09-Oct: Skindles, Maidenhead
10-Oct: Croydon Greyhound
13-Oct: Swansea University
15-Oct: Maidstone Polytechnic
16-Oct: Birmingham University
17-Oct: Roundhouse, London
28-Oct: Kings Hall, Derby
30-Oct: Vale Hall, Aylesbury
02-Nov: Winter Gardens, Bournemouth
03-Nov: Fiesta Club, Plymouth
05-Nov: Edinburgh University
06-Nov: Sunderland Polytechnic
07-Nov: King George's Hall, Blackburn
12-Nov: Town Gate Theatre, Basildon
13-Nov: Strathclyde University, Glasgow
15-Nov: Tiffany's, Hull
19-Nov: Corn Exchange, Cambridge
20-Nov: College of Education, Hitchin
27-Nov: Bath University
04-Dec: Leicester University
08-Dec: Brunel University, Uxbridge
09-Dec: Coatham Bowl, Redcar
10-Dec: Nottingham Trent Polytechnic
11-Dec: City Hall, St Albans

On Track series

Barclay James Harvest – Keith and Monica Domone 978-1-78952-067-5
The Beatles – Andrew Wild 978-1-78952-009-5
The Beatles Solo 1969-1980 – Andrew Wild 978-1-78952-030-9
Blue Oyster Cult – Jacob Holm-Lupo 978-1-78952-007-1
Kate Bush – Bill Thomas 978-1-78952-097-2
The Clash – Nick Assirati 978-1-78952-077-4
Crosby, Stills and Nash – Andrew Wild 978-1-78952-039-2
Deep Purple and Rainbow 1968-79 – Steve Pilkington 978-1-78952-002-6
Dire Straits – Andrew Wild 978-1-78952-044-6
Dream Theater – Jordan Blum 978-1-78952-050-7
Emerson Lake and Palmer – Mike Goode 978-1-78952-000-2
Fairport Convention – Kevan Furbank 978-1-78952-051-4
Genesis – Stuart MacFarlane 978-1-78952-005-7
Gentle Giant – Gary Steel 978-1-78952-058-3
Hawkwind – Duncan Harris 978-1-78952-052-1
Iron Maiden – Steve Pilkington 978-1-78952-061-3
Jethro Tull – Jordan Blum 978-1-78952-016-3
Elton John in the 1970s – Peter Kearns 978-1-78952-034-7
Gong – Kevan Furbank 978-1-78952-082-8
Iron Maiden – Steve Pilkington 978-1-78952-061-3
Judas Priest – John Tucker 978-1-78952-018-7
Kansas – Kevin Cummings 978-1-78952-057-6
Aimee Mann – Jez Rowden 978-1-78952-036-1
Joni Mitchell – Peter Kearns 978-1-78952-081-1
The Moody Blues – Geoffrey Feakes 978-1-78952-042-2
Mike Oldfield – Ryan Yard 978-1-78952-060-6
Queen – Andrew Wild 978-1-78952-003-3
Renaissance – David Detmer 978-1-78952-062-0
The Rolling Stones 1963-80 – Steve Pilkington 978-1-78952-017-0
Steely Dan – Jez Rowden 978-1-78952-043-9
Thin Lizzy – Graeme Stroud 978-1-78952-064-4
Toto – Jacob Holm-Lupo 978-1-78952-019-4
U2 – Eoghan Lyng 978-1-78952-078-1
UFO – Richard James 978-1-78952-073-6
The Who – Geoffrey Feakes 978-1-78952-076-7
Roy Wood and the Move – James R Turner 978-1-78952-008-8
Van Der Graaf Generator – Dan Coffey 978-1-78952-031-6
Yes – Stephen Lambe 978-1-78952-001-9
Frank Zappa 1966 to 1979 – Eric Benac 978-1-78952-033-0
10CC – Peter Kearns 978-1-78952-054-5

Decades Series
Pink Floyd In The 1970s – Georg Purvis 978-1-78952-072-9
Marillion in the 1980s – Nathaniel Webb 978-1-78952-065-1

On Screen series
Carry On... – Stephen Lambe 978-1-78952-004-0
David Cronenberg – Patrick Chapman 978-1-78952-071-2
Doctor Who: The David Tennant Years – Jamie Hailstone 978-1-78952-066-8
Monty Python – Steve Pilkington 978-1-78952-047-7
Seinfeld Seasons 1 to 5 – Stephen Lambe 978-1-78952-012-5

Other Books
Derek Taylor: For Your Radioactive Children – Andrew Darlington
978-1-78952-
Jon Anderson and the Warriors - the road to Yes – David Watkinson
978-1-78952-059-0
Tommy Bolin: In and Out of Deep Purple – Laura Shenton
978-1-78952-070-5
Maximum Darkness – Deke Leonard 978-1-78952-048-4
Maybe I Should've Stayed In Bed – Deke Leonard 978-1-78952-053-8
The Twang Dynasty – Deke Leonard 978-1-78952-049-1

and many more to come!

Would you like to write for Sonicbond Publishing?

At Sonicbond Publishing we are always on the look-out for authors, particularly for our two main series:

On Track. Mixing fact with in depth analysis, the On Track series examines the work of a particular musical artist or group. All genres are considered from easy listening and jazz to 60s soul to 90s pop, via rock and metal.

On Screen. This series looks at the world of film and television. Subjects considered include directors, actors and writers, as well as entire television and film series. As with the On Track series, we balance fact with analysis.

While professional writing experience would, of course, be an advantage the most important qualification is to have real enthusiasm and knowledge of your subject. First-time authors are welcomed, but the ability to write well in English is essential.

Sonicbond Publishing has distribution throughout Europe and North America, and all books are also published in E-book form. Authors will be paid a royalty based on sales of their book.

Further details are available from www.sonicbondpublishing.co.uk. To contact us, complete the contact form there or email info@sonicbondpublishing.co.uk